cool quick summer microwaving

microwave cooking library®

by barbara methven

microwave cooking library®

Make summer living easy! *Cool Quick Summer Microwaving* is an idea book for cool cooking. It includes meals to make ahead in the cool of the day, dishes to tempt heat-jaded appetites and cool summer treats. It also features information on buying and using homegrown produce and fresh herbs, plus menus and recipes for summer events, like backyard entertaining, portable picnics, and foolproof barbecues that combine the best features of both microwave and grill. A glance at the tempting photographs will show what the microwave oven can do without heating up the cook or the kitchen.

Barbara Methven

Barbara Methven

CREDITS:
Design & Production: Cy DeCosse Incorporated
Senior Art Director: Lisa Rosenthal
Art Director: David Schelitzche
Project Director: Peggy Ramette
Project Managers: Holly Clements, Ann Schlachter
Home Economists: Peggy Ramette, Ann Stuart
Assistant Home Economist: Sue Brue
Dietitian: Patricia D. Godfrey. R.D.
Consultants: Lynne Rosetto Kasper, Starla Krause
Editors: Janice Cauley, Bernice Maehren
Production Director: Jim Bindas
Assistant Production Managers: Julie Churchill, Amelia Merz
Typesetting: Kevin D. Frakes, Linda Schloegel
Production Staff: Joe Fahey, Melissa Grabanski, Kim Huntley, Mark Jacobson, Yelena Konrardy, Scott Lamoureux, Daniel Meyers, Greg Wallace, Nik Wogstad
Studio Manager: Cathleen Shannon
Assistant Studio Manager: Rebecca DaWald
Director of Photography: Tony Kubat
Photographers: Phil Aarrestad, Graham Brown, Rex Irmen, Tony Kubat, John Lauenstein, Bill Lindner, Mark Macemon, Mette Nielsen, Cathleen Shannon
Food Stylists: Sue Brue, Bobbette Destiche, Lynn Lohmann, Amy Peterson
Color Separations: Scantrans
Printing: R. R. Donnelley & Sons (0390)

CY DE COSSE INCORPORATED
Chairman: Cy DeCosse
President: James B. Maus
Executive Vice President: William B. Jones

Library of Congress Cataloging-in-Publication Data

Methven, Barbara.
  Cool quick summer microwaving / by Barbara Methven.

  p. cm. — (Microwave cooking library)

  ISBN 0-86573-568-9 :
  1. Microwave cookery. I. Title. II. Series.
TX832.M3917 1990
641.5'882 — dc20

89-28535
CIP

Contents

What You Need to Know Before You Start

Many summer activities involve food—picnics in the park, porch suppers, family reunions, a trip to the beach or weekend cabin. Summertime usually means it is either too hot to cook or too glorious outdoors to be in the kitchen.

Even people who have plenty of time to cook prefer a microwave oven for summer cooking. A conventional oven and range top not only take longer to cook the food, but make cooking uncomfortable because they heat up the kitchen. The microwave oven heats the food, not the cook or the kitchen.

Cool Quick Summer Microwaving features fruit and vegetable charts to help you plan for peak availability and quality of fresh produce. Another chart suggests uses for fresh herbs you find at the market or grow on a sunny windowsill. The book provides information on food storage and safety, and shows you how to pack a picnic cooler.

Beverages & Soups

Cold beverages quench thirst, and cold soups wake up lazy summer appetites. Try the spectacular Icy Ideas—dress up special drinks with special ice cubes, or serve food attractively and keep it cold at the same time.

Salads & Sandwiches

Summer is salad season. This section offers a treasury of tempting recipes, including many different potato salads; molded salads for a main dish, side dish or dessert; plus pasta and fruit salads. Summery sandwiches include variations on old favorites and lettuce bundles for a light meal without bread.

Centerpiece Salads reflect the bounty of early, middle and late summer. These picture platters double as centerpiece and salad course. For main dish variety, add meat or cheese to the early or late seasonal salad. The midsummer fruit salad can be served as a dessert.

Cookouts

Try the hottest idea since the backyard grill. Micro-grilling combines the juicy tenderness of microwaved foods with a distinctive barbecue flavor. Try a complete meal of micro-grilled meats, vegetables and fruits.

Entrées & Side Dishes

Even when served hot, these dishes are quick and cool to cook. Most also make cool eating, since you can prepare them ahead and serve them chilled. Fresh summer produce adds sparkling flavor to both entrées and side dishes.

Sweets

You will find your favorite summer desserts here, plus some refreshing sauces. This section features Quick Pick-Me-Ups. Store these quick-to-make treats in the refrigerator or freezer—no serving dishes needed, they're ready-to-go.

Menus

We've designed menus for special summer occasions—picnics and portable meals, backyard barbecues, porch suppers or light meals that are easy to prepare and tempting to eat during a heat wave. Microwave many of these a day in advance or in the cool of morning; all of them, in minimal time.

Summer Food Safety

In hot weather, shopping for food demands extra caution to prevent spoilage. When you have several errands to run, make the supermarket your last stop before heading home. If plans include a leisurely stroll through the farmers' market, do that before you purchase the more perishable meat, poultry, seafood or dairy products. Never leave perishables in a hot car.

Keep Food Fresh & Cool

Store foods at proper temperature as soon as you get home. Refrigerate eggs immediately and use within a week. Many homegrown fruits and vegetables will lose their fresh-picked flavor if they stand out on the kitchen counter too long.

Hamburger, which has a lot of surfaces exposed to bacteria, can spoil rapidly. Handle it as little as possible, keep it well chilled and use it within two days of purchase. Serve hamburger for a backyard barbecue, where it can go directly from refrigerator to grill. For a cookout away from home, choose a less perishable meat.

Serve Food Piping Hot or Icy Cold

Bacteria that cause food poisoning thrive at temperatures between 60°F and 125°F. Internal temperatures above 165°F or below 40°F kill, or at least retard the growth of, bacteria. Even in winter, foods should never be left at room temperature for more than two hours.

To keep hot foods safe, serve them as soon as they are ready. Cooked eggs and foods made with eggs should be eaten or refrigerated right after preparation.

Refrigerate leftovers promptly. To serve them, cover them and reheat thoroughly in your microwave oven.

Using the barbecue team of microwave oven and grill ensures that food will be cooked through when the surface is browned. Wind and outside temperatures can affect cooking times, so follow recipe directions and doneness tests carefully, and start the grill before you microwave the food.

Cold foods should be chilled thoroughly as soon as they are prepared. To cool foods rapidly after cooking, spread them in a shallow pan or divide them into several small serving dishes, and refrigerate.

Mayonnaise in meat, fish, egg, potato or pasta salads will not increase the risk of food poisoning. The danger comes from refrigerating the salad in a large mass. This does not allow the center to cool rapidly and gives bacteria time to multiply in a warm environment.

Serve cold foods in well-chilled dishes. For additional cold and an attractive presentation, place the dish in a bed of crushed ice.

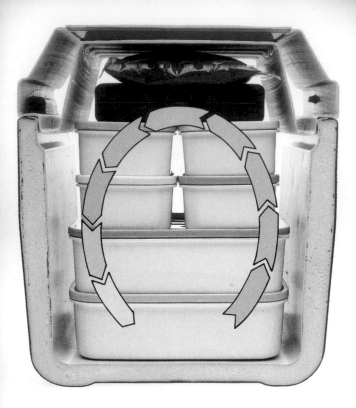

Place refrigerant packs on top of food in cooler. Warm air rises from bottom of cooler and hits ice or refrigerant packs. Air cools and recycles.

Keeping Summer Picnic Foods Cold

Refrigerate food at least six hours to chill it thoroughly. Well-chilled food stays at safe temperatures longer and helps cool the cooler, so ice and ice packs stay frozen longer as well.

Thoroughly chill canned or bottled soft drinks before packing them in the cooler. A layer of warm drinks at the bottom of the cooler will draw cold from perishable items.

If you are using block ice for long-term cooling, place it in the cooler about an hour before you start packing. This lowers the temperature in the cooler, so you can move cold foods and beverages from the refrigerator to a well-chilled space without risk of warming.

How Coolers Keep Food Cold

Coolers made of plastic or metal last for years. With a 25-pound block of ice, either will retain cold for 3 days. Styrofoam® coolers come in a variety of shapes and sizes. They have half the insulation value of metal or plastic. Use them for short-term cooling where light weight is important.

Three Ways to Keep Food Cold

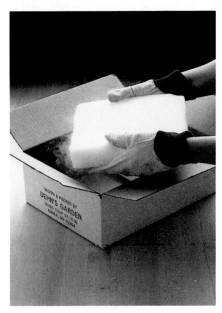

Ice cubes, tightly sealed in bags, will keep chilled food cold for a short trip to a picnic area. Block ice lasts for hours but occupies a lot of cooler space.

Refrigerant and gel packs can be refrozen and reused. Place them in the freezer overnight or at least 8 hours before using. Gel packs are satisfactory for short periods of 4 hours or less. Choose refrigerant packs for longer-lasting cold.

Dry ice will keep food cold for days. Buy dry ice packed in a cardboard box to protect hands and food from freezing. Never handle dry ice with your bare hands or place it directly on food containers; wear heavy gloves or use tongs.

How to Pack a Picnic Cooler

Pack the food in leakproof, spill-proof containers with tight lids, such as plastic storage containers, ice cream pails, or deli packs. To help hold the chill, use containers that fit together compactly without a lot of open air space.

Pack nonperishable items, such as soft drinks, on the bottom; then add a layer of perishables.

Place ice or frozen refrigerant packs directly on top of containers of perishable food. Double the layer of refrigerant packs at top of cooler to keep food cold longer.

Fresh-picked Summer Produce

The following charts divide the growing season into early, middle and late stages. Although spring comes earlier in the South than it does in New England, produce matures in a similar sequence. For example, homegrown rhubarb appears in some gardens in March and others in May, but it is one of the early spring fruits in any area.

Fruits and vegetables that require special growing conditions or a long season to develop will not be available as "homegrown" in all climates. However, the shipped-in items will be plentiful and reasonably priced during the peak of harvest.

Some types of produce, like grapes and lettuce, include several varieties and have extended seasons. Because of varietal and regional differences, it is difficult to identify a single peak season.

Color Key

Fruits		Vegetables	
☐	Available	☐	Available
■	Peak	▦	Peak

Fruit Availability Chart

Fruits	Early Season	Midseason	Late Season
Apples			
Apricots			
Avocados			
Blackberries			
Blueberries			
Cherries			
Grapes			
Melons			
Nectarines			
Peaches			
Pears			
Plums			
Raspberries			
Rhubarb			
Strawberries			

Vegetable Availability Chart

Vegetables	Early Season	Midseason	Late Season
Artichokes			
Asparagus			
Beans			
Beets			
Broccoli			
Brussels Sprouts			
Cabbage			
Carrots			
Cauliflower			
Corn			
Cucumber			
Eggplant			
Lettuce*			
Onions, Dry			
Onions, Green			
Parsnips			
Peas			
Peppers			
Potatoes			
Radishes			
Spinach			
Squash, Summer			
Swiss Chard			
Tomatoes			
Turnips			

*Some varieties of lettuce available all year round.

Basil

Summer Herbs

The fresh herbs of summer can be used to season foods with lively, subtle flavor. Take advantage of their abundance and garnish dishes with sprigs of herbs, using the same ones you use to flavor the food. The following chart suggests herbs and foods that complement each other. Substitute one tablespoon of fresh herbs for one teaspoon of dried herbs in recipes.

Herb	Use In
Basil	Salads, eggplant, green beans, navy beans, onions, any dish containing tomatoes, zucchini, soups, shrimp, fish, beef, pork, veal, lamb, sausage, cheese, eggs, pesto, pasta, seasoned butter, tomato sauce
Chervil (French parsley)	Salads, cabbage, carrots, peas, all roast meats, poultry, eggs, cream sauces
Chives, leaves and flowers	Salads, cucumbers, potatoes, soups, cream cheese
Cilantro (Chinese parsley)	Salads, avocados, tomatoes, legumes, lentils, soups, stews, lamb, poultry, yogurt dishes, couscous, rice
Dill	Salads, cucumbers, green beans, potatoes, fish, cottage cheese, yogurt and sour cream dishes, cream sauce
Marjoram	Salads, lima beans, mushrooms, soups, crab, fish, pot roast, pork, beef, veal, cheese, eggs, brown and cream sauces
Mint	Salads, carrots, cucumbers, peas, potatoes, zucchini, melon, peaches, strawberries, lamb, yogurt dishes
Oregano	Salads, broccoli, cabbage, eggplant, lentils, soups, pork, lamb, sausage, eggs, pasta and tomato sauces
Parsley	Salads, carrots, peas, potatoes, soups, stews, fish, beef, lamb, veal, eggs, tabbouleh, bordelaise sauce, butter, pesto
Rosemary	Eggplant, onions, potatoes, legumes, soups, fish, beef, pork, veal, lamb, poultry, eggs, breads
Sage	Eggplant, onions, tomatoes, legumes, soups, fish, poultry, cottage cheese, eggs, butter sauce for pasta
Summer Savory	Salads, green beans, squash, legumes, lentils, soups, fish, pork, veal, poultry, eggs, rice
Tarragon	Salads, mushrooms, peas, potatoes, soups, fish, veal, poultry, eggs, béarnaise sauce
Thyme	Beets, carrots, onions, soups, stews, pot roast, pork, poultry, lamb, veal, sausage, cottage cheese

Chervil

Chives

Cilantro

Dill

Marjoram

Rosemary

Sage

Mint

Summer Savory

Oregano

Tarragon

Parsley

Thyme

Ice-cold Beverages & Soups

Dark Sweet Cherry-Vanilla Soup

Icy Ideas

Ice Cube Ideas ▶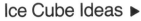

Fruits (whole strawberries;
kiwifruit pieces; blueberries;
grapes; raspberries; cherries;
star fruit; orange, lemon or
lime slices or zest; mandarin
orange segments)
Edible flowers and fresh herbs
(nasturtium, viola, marigold,
or pansy blossoms; rose
petals; mint or lemon balm
leaves)
3 to 4 cups distilled water

32 cubes

In each section of two 16-cube
ice cube trays, place 1 or more
of the fruits and flowers. Fill trays
with water. Freeze overnight. Remove cubes from tray and store
in large plastic food-storage bags.

For each serving, fill glass with
cubes. Pour lemon-lime soda, carbonated water, wine, tea or any
fruit-based beverage over cubes.

Nutritional information not
listed because amounts are
negligible.

Fresh Melon Ice Cubes ▲

4 cups cubed seeded
    watermelon, cantaloupe or
    honeydew melon (1-inch
    cubes, about 2 to 2¼ lbs.)

16 cubes

Per Serving:	
Calories:	28
Protein:	1 g.
Carbohydrate:	7 g.
Fat:	—
Cholesterol:	—
Sodium:	7 mg.
Exchanges:	½ fruit

In food processor or blender, process melon until smooth. Pour into
16-cube ice cube tray. Freeze overnight. Remove cubes from tray and
store in large plastic food-storage bag.

For each serving, fill glass with cubes. Pour fruit juice, carbonated
water or alcoholic beverages over cubes.

Fresh Pineapple-Banana Ice Cubes: Follow recipe above, except
substitute 3 cups peeled and cubed (1-inch cubes) fresh pineapple
and 1 cup fresh banana chunks for melon. Pour club soda, orange
juice or iced tea over cubes.

Flowers & Ice Serving Bowl

Crushed ice
1 large and 1 medium heavy
clear glass bowl
Edible flowers (pansy, sweet
william, rose petals and
buds, nasturtium blossoms)
English ivy leaves or branches
Chilled distilled water

Place enough crushed ice in bottom of large bowl to elevate smaller bowl in center. Place 1-cup measure or other heavy object in center of smaller bowl to weight bowl down.

How to Make Flowers & Ice Serving Bowl

Fill area between 2 bowls with more crushed ice, randomly placing flowers and ivy against sides of bowl and packing with crushed ice to hold in place. Pour chilled water between bowls, filling to top of large bowl. Freeze until firm, about 8 hours or overnight.

Let stand at room temperature for 5 minutes to loosen center bowl. Remove center bowl. Return large bowl to freezer until serving time. Fill smaller bowl with cold salads, soups, fresh fruit or ice cream balls. Place on ice to serve.

Iced Decanter

1 empty wine bottle, rinsed
1 empty milk carton (½ gal.), rinsed
Crushed ice
Rosebuds or flower petals (pansy, nasturtium, sweet william)
English ivy branches
Chilled distilled water

Center wine bottle in milk carton. Fill area between bottle and carton with crushed ice, randomly placing flowers and ivy against sides of carton and packing with crushed ice to hold in place. Add distilled water, filling to top of ice.

Invert 1-cup measure over top of bottle to weight bottle down. Freeze until firm, about 8 hours or overnight.

Tear carton from ice block. Wrap base with cloth napkin. Using funnel, fill bottle with desired beverage.

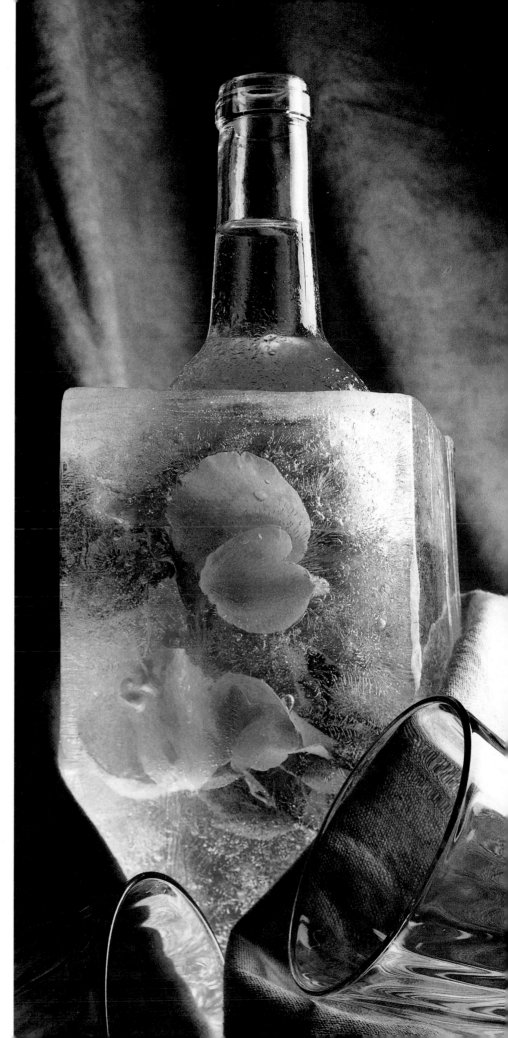

Beverages

Minted Iced Tea ▶

4 cups hot water
1 cup fresh mint leaves
4 tea bags

4 servings

In 8-cup measure, combine water and mint leaves. Cover with plastic wrap. Microwave at High for 6 to 11 minutes, or until mixture begins to boil, stirring once.

Add tea bags and let steep for 5 minutes. Remove tea bags. Strain tea into serving pitcher. Discard mint leaves. Cover with plastic wrap and let cool to room temperature. Serve over ice. Garnish with fresh mint, if desired.

Per Serving:			
Calories:	5	Cholesterol:	—
Protein:	—	Sodium:	—
Carbohydrate:	1 g.	Exchanges:	free
Fat:	—		

Citrus Cinnamon Tea

4 cups hot water
1 can (6 oz.) frozen orange juice concentrate
1 tablespoon sugar
1 cinnamon stick
4 tea bags
1 orange, thinly sliced
1 lemon, thinly sliced
1 lime, thinly sliced

5 servings

In 8-cup measure, combine water, concentrate, sugar and cinnamon stick. Cover with plastic wrap. Microwave at High for 8 to 10 minutes, or until very hot. Stir to dissolve sugar.

Add tea bags and let steep for 5 minutes. Remove tea bags. Cover with plastic wrap and let cool to room temperature. Strain to remove pulp, if desired.

In large pitcher, layer ice cubes with orange, lemon and lime slices. Just before serving, pour tea over cubes. Serve immediately.

Per Serving:			
Calories:	101	Cholesterol:	—
Protein:	1 g.	Sodium:	2 mg.
Carbohydrate:	25 g.	Exchanges:	1½ fruit
Fat:	—		

Iced Mocha Coffee

4 cups hot water
1 tablespoon plus 2 teaspoons instant coffee crystals
1 tablespoon packed brown sugar
2 tablespoons chocolate-flavored syrup

4 servings

Place water in 8-cup measure. Cover with plastic wrap. Microwave at High for 6 to 11 minutes, or until water begins to boil.

Add coffee crystals and sugar. Stir to dissolve. Add chocolate syrup. Stir. Cover with plastic wrap and let cool to room temperature.

Pack tall glasses with ice. Pour coffee over ice. Serve immediately.

Per Serving:			
Calories:	39	Cholesterol:	—
Protein:	—	Sodium:	8 mg.
Carbohydrate:	10 g.	Exchanges:	½ fruit
Fat:	—		

Old-fashioned Limeade Concentrate ▶

- 1 cup fresh lime juice (about 8 limes)
- 1 cup sugar
  Water

To serve:

- 2½ cups cold water
- ½ cup sugar
- 1 lime, thinly sliced

8 servings

In 8-cup measure, combine juice and 1 cup sugar. Add water to equal 3 cups. Microwave at High for 6 to 8 minutes, or until mixture begins to boil and sugar is dissolved, stirring once.

Freeze in 1½-cup amounts in 1-pint plastic freezer storage bags. Freeze up to 6 months.

To make 1 quart of limeade, remove concentrate from 1 bag and place in 8-cup measure. Cover. Microwave at High for 2½ to 3½ minutes, or until defrosted, stirring once to break apart.

Place defrosted limeade concentrate in serving pitcher. Add cold water, ½ cup sugar and the lime slices. Mix well.

Fill serving glasses with ice and fresh mint leaves, if desired. Pour limeade over ice.

Old-fashioned Lemonade: Follow recipe above, except substitute 1 cup fresh lemon juice (about 6 lemons) for limes. When preparing lemonade, reduce added sugar to ¼ cup.

Per Serving:	
Calories:	155
Protein:	—
Carbohydrate:	41 g.
Fat:	—
Cholesterol:	—
Sodium:	1 mg.
Exchanges:	2½ fruit

◄ Raspberry Spritzer

1 pkg. (16 oz.) frozen
   unsweetened raspberries
¼ cup sugar
2 tablespoons lemon juice
2 tablespoons Triple Sec or
   orange juice
   Carbonated water, lemon-
   lime soda, champagne or
   spumanti, chilled

12 servings

In 2-quart casserole, combine raspberries, sugar, lemon juice and Triple Sec. Mix well. Cover. Microwave at High for 5 to 7 minutes, or until raspberries are defrosted and sugar is dissolved, stirring once.

In food processor or blender, process raspberry mixture until smooth. Strain into 4-cup measure. Discard seeds.

In 12-oz. glass, place 2 tablespoons raspberry mixture. Add 1 cup carbonated water. Mix well. Cover and refrigerate remaining mixture no longer than 1 month.

Strawberry Spritzer: Follow recipe above, except substitute 1 pkg. (16 oz.) frozen unsweetened strawberries for raspberries.

Black Raspberry Spritzer: Follow recipe above, except substitute 1 pkg. (10 oz.) frozen unsweetened black raspberries for raspberries.

Per Serving:	
Calories:	36
Protein:	—
Carbohydrate:	9 g.
Fat:	—
Cholesterol:	—
Sodium:	1 mg.
Exchanges:	½ fruit

Very Berry Punch & Ice Ring

2 cups crushed ice
1 cup fresh blueberries
1 cup fresh raspberries
1 cup fresh sliced strawberries
2 bottles (32 oz. each) cran-raspberry drink, chilled, divided

2 cups hot water
1 pkg. (3 oz.) raspberry or black raspberry gelatin
3 bottles (10 oz. each) raspberry or strawberry soda, chilled

16 servings

Per Serving:			
Calories:	129	Cholesterol:	—
Protein:	1 g.	Sodium:	23 mg.
Carbohydrate:	32 g.	Exchanges:	2 fruit
Fat:	—		

How to Make Very Berry Punch & Ice Ring

Place ice in 6½-cup ring mold. Layer ½ cup blueberries, ½ cup raspberries and the strawberries over ice. Repeat layering with remaining berries. Pour 2½ cups cran-raspberry drink over fruit. Refrigerate remaining drink. Freeze mold at least 8 hours or overnight.

Place water in 4-cup measure. Cover with plastic wrap. Microwave at High for 4 to 5 minutes, or until water boils. Add gelatin. Stir until dissolved. Cool slightly. Pour into punch bowl. Add remaining drink and the soda.

Dip mold into warm water for 10 to 15 seconds. Carefully unmold ice ring and place fruit-side-up in punch bowl.

Tropical Fruit Punch & Ice Ring

2 cups crushed ice
1 can (20 oz.) pineapple tidbits, drained
15 maraschino cherries with stems
7 lime slices (¼ inch thick)
9½ cups pine-orange-guava juice or pine-passion-banana juice, chilled, divided
½ cup nonalcoholic piña colada drink mixer, chilled
1 bottle (33.8 oz.) ginger ale, chilled

16 servings

In medium mixing bowl, combine ice and pineapple. Spoon ice mixture into 6½-cup ring mold. Arrange cherries and lime slices over ice mixture. In 4-cup measure, combine 1½ cups juice and the drink mixer. Pour over fruit. Freeze mold at least 8 hours or overnight.

In punch bowl, combine remaining 8 cups juice and the ginger ale. Dip mold into warm water for 10 to 15 seconds. Carefully unmold ice ring and place fruit-side-up in punch bowl.

Per Serving:			
Calories:	137	Cholesterol:	—
Protein:	1 g.	Sodium:	2 mg.
Carbohydrate:	34 g.	Exchanges:	2 fruit
Fat:	—		

Strawberry-Rhubarb Soup

1 pkg. (16 oz.) frozen sliced
   rhubarb
1 cup water
½ cup sugar

1 pkg. (16 oz.) frozen
   unsweetened whole
   strawberries
½ cup whipping cream
½ cup sour cream

6 servings

Per Serving:			
Calories:	214	Cholesterol:	36 mg.
Protein:	2 g.	Sodium:	21 mg.
Carbohydrate:	27 g.	Exchanges:	2 fruit, 2 fat
Fat:	12 g.		

How to Microwave Strawberry-Rhubarb Soup

Combine rhubarb, water and sugar in 3-quart casserole. Mix well. Cover. Microwave at High for 10 to 14 minutes, or until rhubarb is very tender, stirring once.

Add strawberries. Mix well. Let stand for 3 to 5 minutes, or until strawberries are defrosted. In food processor or blender, process rhubarb mixture until smooth.

Set aside 3 cups of processed rhubarb mixture. Add whipping cream and sour cream to remaining 2 cups of mixture. Process until smooth. Cover. Chill until cold.

Measure ½ cup of each mixture for each serving and simultaneously pour into bowl. Using wooden pick, swirl the two mixtures together.

Watermelon-Lime Soup ▶

1 cup hot water
3 tablespoons honey
1 teaspoon grated lime peel
2 tablespoons fresh lime juice
6 cups cubed seeded
    watermelon (½-inch cubes)

4 to 6 servings

In 2-quart casserole, place water, honey, lime peel and juice. Cover. Microwave at High for 2 to 3 minutes, or until honey dissolves, stirring once.

In food processor or blender, place half of juice mixture and half of watermelon. Process until smooth. Pour into large serving bowl. Repeat with remaining juice mixture and watermelon. Cover with plastic wrap. Chill at least 2 hours, or until cold. Garnish each serving with melon balls and lime slices, if desired.

Per Serving:	
Calories:	85
Protein:	1 g.
Carbohydrate:	21 g.
Fat:	1 g.
Cholesterol:	—
Sodium:	4 mg.
Exchanges:	1½ fruit

Cold Lemon-Blueberry Soup

1 pkg. (16 oz.) frozen
    unsweetened blueberries
2 cups water
1 can (6 oz.) frozen lemonade
    concentrate
1 cinnamon stick
½ cup whipping cream
½ cup sour cream

4 to 6 servings

In 3-quart casserole, combine blueberries, water, concentrate and cinnamon stick. Cover. Microwave at High for 12 to 18 minutes, or until mixture is very hot and blueberries are softened, stirring twice.

Strain mixture into large mixing bowl or 8-cup measure. Discard cinnamon stick. Press berries with back of spoon to release pulp. Discard skins. Cover with plastic wrap. Chill at least 4 hours, or until cold.

In large mixing bowl, place whipping cream and sour cream. Beat at medium speed of electric mixer until combined. Gradually add blueberry mixture to cream mixture, while continuing to beat at medium speed. Beat until combined.

Per Serving:				
Calories:	219		Cholesterol:	36 mg.
Protein:	1 g.		Sodium:	20 mg.
Carbohydrate:	29 g.		Exchanges:	2 fruit, 2 fat
Fat:	12 g.			

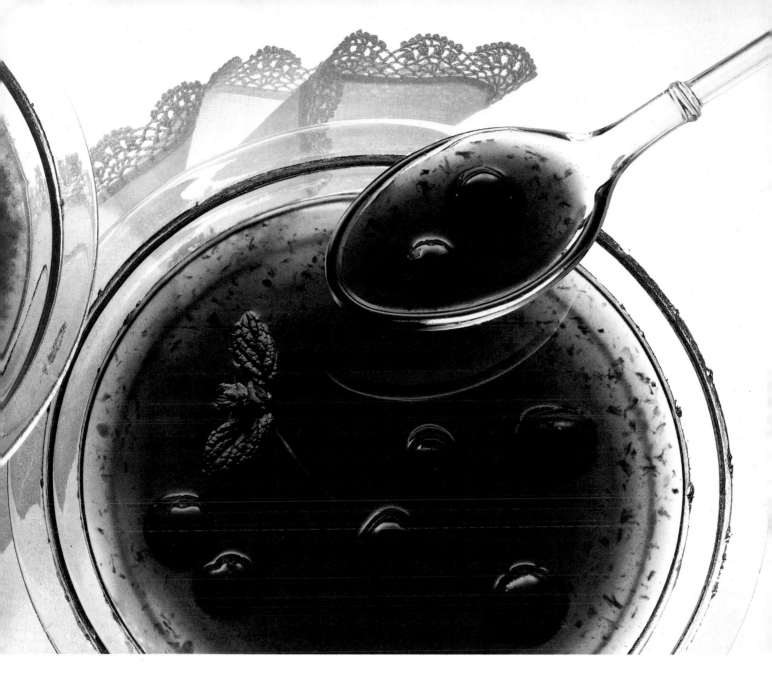

Dark Sweet Cherry-Vanilla Soup ▲

3 cups hot water
1 pkg. (16 oz.) frozen pitted
   dark sweet cherries
¼ cup sugar
1 whole vanilla bean
3 tablespoons cornstarch
3 tablespoons cold water

4 to 6 servings

In 3-quart casserole, combine hot water, cherries, sugar and vanilla bean. Cover. Microwave at High for 12 to 20 minutes, or until mixture begins to boil and sugar dissolves, stirring once or twice. Remove and discard vanilla bean. Strain mixture into large serving bowl, pressing cherries with back of spoon to release pulp. Discard skins. Set mixture aside.

In small bowl, blend cornstarch and cold water until smooth. Add to reserved mixture. Mix well. Microwave at High for 4 to 6 minutes, or until soup is thickened and translucent, stirring every 2 minutes. Chill at least 4 hours, or until cold. Garnish each serving with fresh cherries and a dollop of sour cream, if desired.

Per Serving:			
Calories:	101	Cholesterol:	—
Protein:	1 g.	Sodium:	—
Carbohydrate:	24 g.	Exchanges:	1½ fruit
Fat:	1 g.		

Iced Tomato Dill Bisque

4 medium tomatoes (about 2 lbs.)
4 cups hot water
4 cups ice water
1 can (14½ oz.) ready-to-serve chicken broth
¼ cup sliced green onions
2 tablespoons snipped fresh dill weed or 1 teaspoon dried dill weed
1 tablespoon olive oil
1 tablespoon snipped fresh parsley
¼ teaspoon salt
½ cup whipping cream

4 to 6 servings

Using sharp knife, cut crossmark on bottom of each tomato. Set aside. Place hot water in 2-quart casserole or 8-cup measure. Cover. Microwave at High for 6 to 11 minutes, or until water boils. Add tomatoes. Let stand for 1½ minutes.

Place ice water in medium mixing bowl. Immerse tomatoes briefly in ice water. Core and peel tomatoes. Cut in half crosswise. Remove and discard seeds. Cut tomatoes into ½-inch chunks.

In 2-quart casserole, place tomatoes, chicken broth, onions, dill, oil, parsley and salt. Mix well. Cover. Microwave at High for 10 to 16 minutes, or until tomatoes are very tender, stirring once or twice.

In food processor or blender, process tomato mixture until smooth. Pour back into 2-quart casserole. Cover. Chill at least 4 hours or overnight. Before serving, stir small amount of tomato mixture into cream. Add back to tomato mixture. Mix well. Garnish each serving with sprigs of fresh dill, if desired.

Per Serving:	
Calories:	127
Protein:	3 g.
Carbohydrate:	7 g.
Fat:	10 g.
Cholesterol:	27 mg.
Sodium:	321 mg.
Exchanges:	1½ vegetable, 2 fat

Carrot Vichyssoise

1 pkg. (3 oz.) cream cheese
1 lb. white potatoes, peeled and thinly sliced (about 3 cups)
2 medium carrots, thinly sliced (about 1 cup)
¼ cup finely chopped onion
¼ cup water
1 tablespoon olive oil
2 teaspoons lemon juice
1 teaspoon curry powder
½ teaspoon salt
⅛ teaspoon pepper
1½ cups milk

6 servings

In small bowl, microwave cream cheese at High for 15 to 30 seconds, or until softened. Set aside.

In 2-quart casserole, combine remaining ingredients, except milk. Mix well. Cover. Microwave at High for 15 to 18 minutes, or until potatoes and carrots are tender, stirring 2 or 3 times.

In food processor or blender, combine potato mixture, milk and cream cheese. Process until smooth. Return potato mixture to 2-quart casserole. Cover. Chill at least 4 hours or overnight. Serve soup garnished with finely shredded carrot, if desired.

TIP: If soup becomes too thick after chilling, gradually beat in ⅓ to ½ cup additional milk for desired consistency.

Per Serving:			
Calories:	159	Cholesterol:	20 mg.
Protein:	5 g.	Sodium:	262 mg.
Carbohydrate:	17 g.	Exchanges:	½ starch, ½ vegetable,
Fat:	9 g.		½ low-fat milk, 1 fat

Green Gazpacho

1 pkg. (10 oz.) frozen peas
2 tablespoons olive oil
2 cloves garlic, minced
1 can (14½ oz.) ready-to-serve chicken broth
1 avocado, peeled and cut into chunks
2 tablespoons lime juice
½ to ¾ teaspoon ground cumin
¼ teaspoon cayenne
2 cups peeled seeded chopped cucumber (about 1 large cucumber)
¼ cup sliced green onions

4 to 6 servings

In 2-quart casserole, combine peas, oil and garlic. Cover. Microwave at High for 6 to 8 minutes, or until peas are defrosted, stirring once.

In food processor or blender, place 1 cup of peas. Set remaining peas aside. Add chicken broth, avocado, lime juice, cumin and cayenne. Process until smooth. Pour puréed mixture back into 2-quart casserole.

Add remaining peas, the cucumber and green onions. Mix well. Cover. Chill at least 2 hours, or until cold. Serve topped with seeded chopped tomato and snipped fresh parsley, if desired.

Per Serving:			
Calories:	152	Cholesterol:	—
Protein:	5 g.	Sodium:	276 mg.
Carbohydrate:	12 g.	Exchanges:	1½ starch, 1 vegetable, 2 fat
Fat:	10 g.		

Fine Herb Soup

  1 leek, cut in half lengthwise
     and rinsed
  3 tablespoons olive oil
  2 tablespoons fresh marjoram
     leaves
  2 tablespoons snipped fresh
     parsley
  2 tablespoons fresh thyme
     leaves
  2 cloves garlic, minced
  ¼ cup plus 2 tablespoons
     all-purpose flour
  ½ teaspoon salt
  ½ teaspoon pepper
  2 cans (14½ oz. each) ready-
     to-serve chicken broth
 1½ cups half-and-half

          4 to 6 servings

Thinly slice leek to yield 1 cup. Reserve any remaining leek for future use. In 3-quart casserole, combine leek, oil, marjoram, parsley, thyme and garlic. Mix well. Cover. Microwave at High for 3 to 4 minutes, or until leek is tender.

Stir in flour, salt and pepper. Blend in broth and half-and-half. Microwave at High for 11 to 16 minutes, or until soup thickens and bubbles, stirring after first 4 minutes, and then every 3 minutes. Cover. Chill 4 hours or overnight.

Per Serving:			
Calories:	206	Cholesterol:	22 mg.
Protein:	6 g.	Sodium:	643 mg.
Carbohydrate:	13 g.	Exchanges:	1 vegetable, ½ whole milk, 2½ fat
Fat:	15 g.		

Cool Summer Salads & Sandwiches

Pasta Salads

Thai-style Shrimp Salad

4	cups plus 2 tablespoons water, divided
2½	oz. uncooked cellophane noodles
3	tablespoons soy sauce
1	tablespoon rice wine vinegar
1	tablespoon sesame oil
1	to 2 teaspoons hot pepper oil

1	pkg. (12 oz.) frozen uncooked medium shrimp, defrosted
1	cup julienne carrot (2 × ⅛-inch strips)
1	medium cucumber, cut in half lengthwise and sliced (¼-inch slices)*
1	cup shredded leaf lettuce

Per Serving:
Calories:	229
Protein:	21 g.
Carbohydrate:	20 g.
Fat:	7 g.
Cholesterol:	146 mg.
Sodium:	910 mg.
Exchanges:	1 starch, 2½ lean meat, 1 vegetable

4 servings

*Before slicing cucumber, remove and discard thin lengthwise strips of peel with zester, if desired.

How to Microwave Thai-style Shrimp Salad

Place 4 cups water in 3-quart casserole. Cover. Microwave at High for 9½ to 13 minutes, or until water begins to boil. Place noodles in water. Cover. Let stand for 10 to 15 minutes, or until noodles are tender. Drain. Cut noodles with scissors into 2-inch lengths. Set noodles aside.

Combine soy sauce, vinegar and oils in 1-cup measure. Blend with whisk. Set aside. In 10-inch square casserole, arrange shrimp in single layer. Cover with plastic wrap. Microwave at 70% (Medium High) for 6 to 7 minutes, or until shrimp are opaque, stirring once. Let stand, covered, for 1 to 2 minutes. Drain. Set aside.

Place carrot strips and the remaining 2 tablespoons water in 2-quart casserole. Cover. Microwave at High for 4 to 6 minutes, or until carrots are tender, stirring once. Drain. Add noodles, the soy sauce mixture and shrimp to carrots. Toss to combine. Cover. Chill at least 2 hours, or until cold. Add cucumber and lettuce. Toss gently and serve immediately.

Mexicali Turkey & Pasta Salad

- 8 oz. uncooked radiatore pasta (pasta nuggets)
- 1 cup green pepper strips (2 × ¼-inch strips)
- 1 cup red pepper strips (2 × ¼-inch strips)
- 2 tablespoons water
- 2 cups shredded cooked turkey
- 1½ cups halved cherry tomatoes
- 1 can (8 oz.) corn, drained
- 1 can (4 oz.) chopped green chilies, drained
- ¼ cup medium or hot salsa
- 2 tablespoons mayonnaise or salad dressing
- 2 tablespoons sour cream
  Leaf lettuce
  Avocado slices

8 servings

Prepare pasta as directed on package. Rinse with cold water. Drain. Place in large mixing bowl. Set aside.

In 1-quart casserole, combine peppers and water. Cover. Microwave at High for 4 to 6 minutes, or until peppers are tender, stirring once. Rinse and drain.

Add cooked peppers, the turkey, tomatoes, corn and chilies to cooked pasta. Toss to combine.

In small mixing bowl, combine salsa, mayonnaise and sour cream. Mix well. Add to pasta mixture. Toss to coat. Serve on lettuce-lined platter. Garnish with avocado slices.

Per Serving:	
Calories:	251
Protein:	16 g.
Carbohydrate:	31 g.
Fat:	8 g.
Cholesterol:	30 mg.
Sodium:	189 mg.
Exchanges:	1½ starch, 1 lean meat, 1½ vegetable, 1 fat

Sesame Noodle Salad

12 oz. uncooked spaghetti
 4 oz. fresh pea pods, sliced
    lengthwise into thin strips
    (about 1 cup)
 ½ cup julienne carrot
    (2 × ⅛-inch strips)
 2 tablespoons water
 ½ cup diagonally sliced green
    onions

Dressing:

 ¾ cup light or regular
    mayonnaise or salad
    dressing
 2 tablespoons sesame oil
 1 tablespoon soy sauce
 ¼ to ½ teaspoon crushed red
    pepper flakes

8 servings

Prepare spaghetti as directed on
package. Rinse with cold water.
Drain. Set aside.

In 1-quart casserole, combine
pea pods, carrot strips and water.
Cover. Microwave at High for 1½
to 3 minutes, or until vegetables
are very hot and colors brighten.
Rinse with cold water. Drain.

In large mixing bowl or salad bowl,
combine cooked spaghetti, the
pea pods and carrot strips, and
onions. Toss to combine. Set aside.

In small mixing bowl, combine
dressing ingredients. Mix well.
Add to spaghetti mixture. Toss to
coat. Cover with plastic wrap. Chill
at least 2 hours, or until cold.

Per Serving:	
Calories:	263
Protein:	6 g.
Carbohydrate:	35 g.
Fat:	11 g.
Cholesterol:	9 mg.
Sodium:	259 mg.
Exchanges:	2 starch, 1 vegetable, 2 fat

Mediterranean Pasta Salad with Lemon Oregano Dressing ▲

 8 oz. uncooked tricolored
    rotini or fusilli
 1 boneless whole chicken
    breast (8 to 10 oz.), skin
    removed
1½ cups seeded chopped
    tomatoes
 1 jar (6 oz.) marinated
    artichoke hearts, drained
    and chopped

 ½ cup sliced black olives
 ½ cup crumbled feta cheese
 ¼ cup snipped fresh parsley
 ¼ cup chopped red onion
 ½ cup olive oil
 3 tablespoons lemon juice
 1 teaspoon dried oregano
    leaves
 ½ teaspoon salt

6 to 8 servings

Prepare rotini as directed on package. Rinse with cold water. Drain.
Set aside.

Place chicken breast on microwave roasting rack. Cover with wax
paper. Microwave at High for 4 to 6 minutes, or until meat is no longer
pink and juices run clear, turning over once. Let stand, covered, for 3
minutes. Cool slightly. Shred chicken into 2 × ¼-inch strips.

In large mixing bowl or salad bowl, combine cooked rotini and chicken,
the tomatoes, artichokes, olives, cheese, parsley and onion. Toss gently
to combine.

In small mixing bowl, combine oil, juice, oregano and salt. Stir with
whisk to blend. Pour over salad ingredients. Toss to coat. Cover with
plastic wrap. Chill at least 4 hours, or until cold.

Per Serving:			
Calories:	330	Cholesterol:	32 mg.
Protein:	14 g.	Sodium:	345 mg.
Carbohydrate:	26 g.	Exchanges:	1 starch, 1 lean meat, 2 vegetable, 3 fat
Fat:	19 g.		

Potato Salads

Farmers' Market Potato Salad ▶

2 lbs. round red or white
 potatoes, peeled and cut into
 ½-inch cubes (about 5 cups)
½ cup water, divided
2 tablespoons vegetable oil
2 tablespoons white vinegar
2 cups fresh broccoli flowerets
1 cup sliced carrots
 (¼-inch slices)
¼ cup mayonnaise or salad
 dressing

¼ cup sour cream
1 tablespoon Dijon mustard
½ teaspoon dried basil leaves
¼ teaspoon salt
¼ teaspoon pepper
1 cup quartered cherry
 tomatoes
½ cup sliced radishes
 (¼-inch slices)

6 servings

In 3-quart casserole, combine potatoes and ¼ cup water. Cover. Microwave at High for 15 to 17 minutes, or until potatoes are tender, stirring once. Drain. Add oil and vinegar. Toss to coat. Set aside.

In 1-quart casserole, combine broccoli, carrots and remaining ¼ cup water. Cover. Microwave at High for 6 to 8 minutes, or until vegetables are tender, stirring once. Drain. Set aside.

In small mixing bowl, combine mayonnaise, sour cream, mustard, basil, salt and pepper. Add mayonnaise mixture, broccoli and carrots, tomatoes and radishes to potatoes. Toss to coat. Cover with plastic wrap. Chill at least 4 hours, or until cold.

Per Serving:			
Calories:	244	Cholesterol:	10 mg.
Protein:	4 g.	Sodium:	241 mg.
Carbohydrate:	26 g.	Exchanges:	1 starch, 1 vegetable, 2½ fat
Fat:	15 g.		

Blue Cheese Potato Salad

2 lbs. new potatoes, quartered
 (about 5 cups)
¼ cup water
2 tablespoons vegetable oil
2 tablespoons white vinegar
½ cup crumbled blue cheese
 (2 oz.)
⅓ cup sour cream
1 tablespoon snipped fresh
 chives
1 teaspoon sugar
¼ teaspoon salt
⅛ teaspoon pepper
6 slices bacon
2 cups torn romaine lettuce
1 cup quartered cherry
 tomatoes

6 servings

In 3-quart casserole, combine potatoes and water. Cover. Microwave at High for 15 to 21 minutes, or until potatoes are tender, stirring once. Drain. Add oil and vinegar. Toss to coat. Set aside.

In small mixing bowl, combine cheese, sour cream, chives, sugar, salt and pepper. Mix well. Add dressing to potatoes. Toss to coat. Cover with plastic wrap. Chill at least 4 hours, or until cold.

Layer 3 paper towels on plate. Arrange bacon on paper towels. Cover with another paper towel. Microwave at High for 3 to 7 minutes, or until bacon is brown and crisp. Let stand for 5 minutes. Crumble.

Add bacon, romaine and tomatoes to potato mixture. Toss gently. Serve immediately.

Per Serving:			
Calories:	286	Cholesterol:	20 mg.
Protein:	8 g.	Sodium:	358 mg.
Carbohydrate:	34 g.	Exchanges:	2 starch, 1 vegetable, 2½ fat
Fat:	14 g.		

Cold German-style Potato Salad

6 slices bacon
2 lbs. new potatoes, quartered (about 5 cups)
½ medium green pepper, thinly sliced
1 small onion, thinly sliced
¼ cup water

Dressing:

⅓ cup vegetable oil
3 tablespoons white vinegar
1 tablespoon plus 1 teaspoon sugar
1 teaspoon celery seed
½ teaspoon salt
¼ teaspoon pepper

6 servings

Layer 3 paper towels on plate. Arrange bacon on paper towels. Cover with another paper towel. Microwave at High for 3 to 7 minutes, or until bacon is brown and crisp. Set aside.

In 2-quart casserole, combine potatoes, green pepper, onion and water. Cover. Microwave at High for 15 to 21 minutes, or until tender, stirring once. Drain. Crumble bacon. Add to potatoes. Set aside.

In 2-cup measure, combine dressing ingredients. Microwave at High for 30 seconds to 1 minute, or until sugar dissolves, stirring twice. Pour over potato mixture. Toss to coat. Cover. Chill 4 hours, or until cold. Serve with slotted spoon.

Per Serving:			
Calories:	294	Cholesterol:	5 mg.
Protein:	5 g.	Sodium:	286 mg.
Carbohydrate:	35 g.	Exchanges:	2 starch, 1 vegetable, 3 fat
Fat:	16 g.		

Traditional Potato Salad ▶

Salad:
- 2 lbs. round red or white potatoes, peeled and cut into ½-inch cubes (about 5 cups)
- ¼ cup water
- 2 hard-cooked eggs, chopped
- ½ cup chopped celery
- ⅓ cup sliced green onions
- 2 tablespoons sliced pimiento-stuffed green olives (optional)

Dressing:
- ½ cup mayonnaise or salad dressing
- ¼ cup sour cream
- 1 tablespoon prepared mustard
- ½ teaspoon celery salt
- ¼ teaspoon garlic powder
- ⅛ teaspoon paprika
- ⅛ teaspoon pepper

Garnish:
- 3 fresh pea pods
- 1 teaspoon water
- 3 thin lengthwise slices carrot

  Leaf lettuce

6 servings

In 2-quart casserole, place potatoes and ¼ cup water. Cover. Microwave at High for 15 to 17 minutes, or until potatoes are very tender, stirring once. Add remaining salad ingredients. Mix well. Set aside.

In small mixing bowl, combine dressing ingredients. Mix well. Add to salad mixture. Toss to coat. Set aside. Line 8 × 4-inch loaf dish with plastic wrap. Set aside.

In small bowl, place pea pods and 1 teaspoon water. Cover with plastic wrap. Microwave at High for 30 to 45 seconds, or until color brightens. Rinse with cold water.

Cut carrot slices into tulip shapes. Cut wedge from one end of each of two pea pods to make leaves. Cut thin lengthwise strips from remaining pea pod to make stems. Arrange garnish in bottom of prepared dish. Top with salad mixture, packing lightly. Cover with plastic wrap and chill at least 4 hours, or until cold. Serve inverted on lettuce-lined platter.

Per Serving:				
Calories:	319	Cholesterol:	107 mg.	
Protein:	6 g.	Sodium:	329 mg.	
Carbohydrate:	33 g.	Exchanges:	2 starch, 3½ fat	
Fat:	19 g.			

Pesto Potato Salad

- 2 lbs. new potatoes, cut into ¼-inch slices (about 5 cups)
- ¼ cup water
- 1 large clove garlic
- 1 cup loosely packed fresh basil leaves
- ⅓ cup freshly grated Parmesan cheese
- ¼ cup olive oil
- ¼ cup packed snipped fresh parsley
- 1 teaspoon grated lemon peel
- ½ teaspoon salt
- ⅓ cup pine nuts
- 1½ cups seeded chopped Roma tomatoes

6 servings

In 3-quart casserole, combine potatoes and water. Cover. Microwave at High for 15 to 17 minutes, or until potatoes are tender, stirring once. Drain. Set aside.

In food processor or blender, process garlic until finely chopped. Add basil, cheese, oil, parsley, lemon peel and salt. Pulse 15 times, or until mixture is coarsely chopped.

Add basil mixture, pine nuts and tomatoes to potatoes. Toss gently to coat. Serve warm, or chill at least 4 hours, or until cold. Before serving, sprinkle salad lightly with freshly grated Parmesan cheese, if desired.

Per Serving:				
Calories:	284	Cholesterol:	4 mg.	
Protein:	7 g.	Sodium:	296 mg.	
Carbohydrate:	35 g.	Exchanges:	2 starch, 1 vegetable, 2½ fat	
Fat:	14 g.			

Molded Salads

Frosted Blueberry Mold

    Vegetable oil
2 cans (16½ oz. each)
    blueberries in heavy syrup,
    undrained
1 cup vanilla ice cream
½ cup cold water
2 envelopes (0.25 oz. each)
    unflavored gelatin
    Whipped cream (optional)
    Grated lemon peel (optional)

10 servings

Brush 5-cup gelatin mold lightly with vegetable oil. Set aside. Place blueberries in large mixing bowl. Set aside.

In small mixing bowl, microwave ice cream at 50% (Medium) for 1 to 2 minutes, or until ice cream is melted and can be stirred smooth, stirring twice. Add to blueberries. Mix well. Set aside.

Place water in 2-cup measure. Sprinkle gelatin over water. Let stand for 5 minutes. Microwave at High for 30 seconds to 1¼ minutes, or until dissolved, stirring once. Add to blueberry mixture. Mix well.

Pour mixture into prepared mold. Chill about 4 hours, or until set. Dip mold into warm water for 30 to 45 seconds. Loosen edges and unmold onto serving plate. Decorate with whipped cream. Sprinkle with lemon peel.

Per Serving:	
Calories:	118
Protein:	2 g.
Carbohydrate:	24 g.
Fat:	2 g.
Cholesterol:	6 mg.
Sodium:	16 mg.
Exchanges:	1½ fruit, ½ fat

Pink Grapefruit Salad with Raspberry Sauce

⅔ cup cold water
2 envelopes (0.25 oz. each) unflavored gelatin
1 can (6 oz.) frozen grapefruit juice concentrate
½ cup sugar
1 pkg. (8 oz.) cream cheese
3 drops red food coloring
2 cups whipping cream
  Vegetable oil

Sauce:
1 pkg. (12 oz.) frozen unsweetened whole raspberries
¼ cup water
2 tablespoons lemon juice
¼ cup sugar
1 tablespoon cornstarch

10 servings

Per Serving:	
Calories:	360
Protein:	5 g.
Carbohydrate:	29 g.
Fat:	26 g.
Cholesterol:	90 mg.
Sodium:	87 mg.
Exchanges:	1½ fruit,
	½ whole milk, 4½ fat

Place ⅔ cup water in 2-cup measure. Sprinkle gelatin over water. Let stand for 5 minutes. Microwave at High for 30 seconds to 1¼ minutes, or until dissolved, stirring once. Set aside.

In 1-quart casserole, microwave concentrate at High for 1 to 2½ minutes, or until defrosted. Add sugar. Mix well. Cover. Microwave at High for 1 to 2 minutes, or until sugar dissolves, stirring once. Add gelatin mixture. Mix well. Set aside.

In large mixing bowl, microwave cream cheese at 50% (Medium) for 1½ to 3 minutes, or until softened. Beat at medium speed of electric mixer until smooth. Gradually beat in juice mixture and food coloring until well blended. Chill about 30 minutes, or until soft-set. In medium mixing bowl, beat whipping cream at high speed of electric mixer until soft peaks form. Fold gently into juice mixture. Brush 5-cup gelatin mold lightly with vegetable oil. Pour mixture into mold. Cover with plastic wrap. Chill 6 hours, or until set.

Place raspberries in 1-quart casserole. Cover. Microwave at High for 4 to 5 minutes, or until raspberries are defrosted, stirring once. Strain raspberries into 4-cup measure, reserving juice. Set raspberries aside.

In small mixing bowl, combine ¼ cup water and the lemon juice. Blend in sugar and cornstarch. Add to raspberry juice. Mix well. Microwave at High for 2½ to 4 minutes, or until mixture is thickened and translucent, stirring twice. Add raspberries to thickened sauce. Mix well. Chill 2 hours, or until cold.

Dip mold into warm water for 45 seconds to 1 minute. Loosen edges and unmold onto serving platter. Spoon sauce over salad.

Summer Melon Salad

Vegetable oil
1 cup puréed honeydew melon
1 cup puréed cantaloupe
¼ cup cold water
1 envelope (0.25 oz.)
   unflavored gelatin
2 cups hot water
1 pkg. (3 oz.) lime gelatin
1 pkg. (3 oz.) orange gelatin
2 cartons (8 oz. each) vanilla-
   flavored low-fat yogurt,
   divided

12 servings

Brush 6-cup gelatin ring mold lightly with vegetable oil. Set aside. Purée honeydew melon; set aside. Purée cantaloupe; set aside. Continue as directed below.

Per Serving:	
Calories:	104
Protein:	4 g.
Carbohydrate:	21 g.
Fat:	1 g.
Cholesterol:	2 mg.
Sodium:	74 mg.
Exchanges:	1½ fruit

How to Microwave Summer Melon Salad

Place ¼ cup cold water in 1-cup measure. Sprinkle unflavored gelatin over water. Let stand for 5 minutes. Microwave at High for 30 seconds to 1¼ minutes, or until dissolved, stirring once. Set aside.

Place hot water in 4-cup measure. Cover with plastic wrap. Microwave at High for 4 to 5 minutes, or until water boils. Pour lime gelatin in medium mixing bowl. Pour orange gelatin in another medium mixing bowl. Set bowls aside.

Pour 1 cup boiling water over lime gelatin. Pour remaining 1 cup boiling water over orange gelatin. Stir both gelatins until dissolved. Add honeydew and 1 carton yogurt to lime gelatin. Stir with whisk until mixture is smooth.

Add cantaloupe and remaining carton yogurt to orange gelatin. Stir with whisk until mixture is smooth. Add 2 tablespoons un-flavored gelatin mixture to each melon mixture. Mix well.

Chill mixtures about 40 minutes to 1 hour, or until soft-set. Pour soft-set honeydew mixture into prepared mold. Top with soft-set cantaloupe mixture. Chill about 4 hours, or until set.

Dip mold into warm water for 30 seconds. Loosen edges and un-mold onto platter. Fill center of mold with melon balls, peach slices and raspberries, if desired.

Molded Shrimp Salad

Vegetable oil
1 lb. medium shrimp, shelled and deveined
¼ cup cold water
1 envelope (0.25 oz.) unflavored gelatin
1 can (10¾ oz.) condensed tomato soup
1 pkg. (8 oz.) cream cheese
¼ cup mayonnaise or salad dressing
¼ teaspoon cayenne
1 cup peeled seeded chopped cucumber
½ cup chopped celery
½ cup chopped green pepper
Leaf lettuce

4 to 6 servings

Brush 5-cup fish-shaped gelatin mold lightly with vegetable oil. Set aside. Arrange shrimp in single layer in 10-inch square casserole. Cover. Microwave at 70% (Medium High) for 5 to 8 minutes, or until shrimp are opaque, stirring once. Let stand, covered, for 1 to 2 minutes. Drain. Set aside.

Place water in 1-cup measure. Sprinkle gelatin over water. Let stand for 5 minutes. Microwave at High for 30 seconds to 1¼ minutes, or until gelatin dissolves, stirring once. Place soup in 1-quart casserole. Stir in gelatin mixture. Microwave at High for 1 to 2 minutes, or until mixture can be stirred smooth. Set aside.

In large mixing bowl, microwave cream cheese at 50% (Medium) for 1½ to 3 minutes, or until softened. Add mayonnaise and cayenne. Beat at medium speed of electric mixer until well blended. Gradually beat in soup mixture until well blended. Stir in shrimp, cucumber, celery and pepper. Chill about 1 hour, or until soft-set. Mix well.

Pour into prepared mold. Cover with plastic wrap. Chill about 4 hours, or until set. Line serving platter with leaf lettuce. Dip mold into warm water for 30 seconds. Loosen edges and unmold onto platter. Decorate as directed below.

Per Serving:			
Calories:	312	Cholesterol:	133 mg.
Protein:	17 g.	Sodium:	613 mg.
Carbohydrate:	10 g.	Exchanges:	2 lean meat, 2 vegetable, 3½ fat
Fat:	23 g.		

How to Decorate Molded Shrimp Salad

Slice 6 radishes thinly to make fish scales. Cut slices in half. Arrange slices, slightly overlapping, over body of fish. Cut 1 cucumber in half lengthwise to make fish tail and fin.

Wrap and reserve half of cucumber for future use. Place remaining half cut-side-down on flat surface. Slice off one end diagonally. Make about 8 thin diagonal slices to within ¼ inch of edge, for tail. Cut from cucumber.

Cut cucumber flesh carefully from skin, leaving ½ inch. Turn every other slice back toward joined end. Repeat for fin.

46

Molded Saffron Rice & Chicken Salad

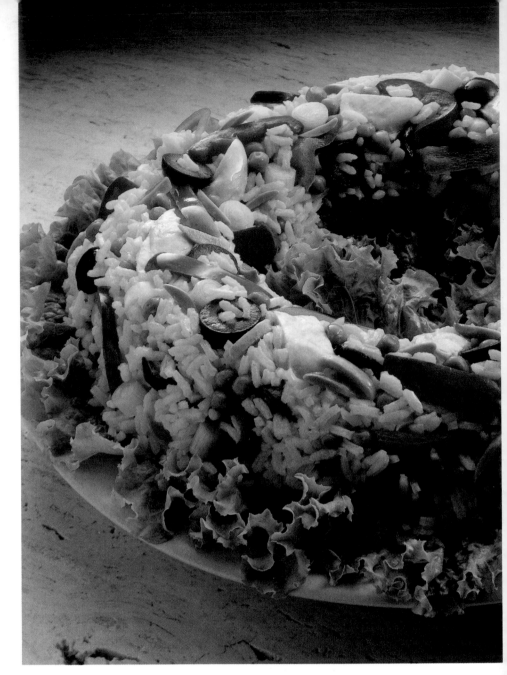

Nonstick vegetable cooking
  spray
1 tablespoon margarine or
  butter
¼ cup slivered almonds
1 boneless whole chicken
  breast (8 to 10 oz.), skin
  removed
  Garlic salt
3 cups hot water
1½ cups uncooked long-grain
  white rice
1 teaspoon instant chicken
  bouillon granules
¼ teaspoon saffron threads,
  crushed
1 cup frozen peas
¾ cup green pepper strips
  (2 × ¼-inch)
¾ cup red pepper strips
  (2 × ¼-inch)
¼ cup water
½ cup sliced black olives
¼ cup sliced green onions
  Leaf lettuce

6 servings

Spray 6-cup glass ring mold with nonstick vege-table cooking spray. Set aside. In 9-inch pie plate, microwave margarine at High for 30 to 45 seconds, or until melted. Stir in almonds, tossing to coat. Microwave at High for 3½ to 5½ minutes, or until light golden brown, stirring every 2 minutes. Set aside.

Place chicken breast on roasting rack. Sprinkle lightly with garlic salt. Cover with wax paper. Micro-wave at High for 4 to 6 minutes, or until meat is no longer pink and juices run clear, turning over once. Let stand, covered, for 3 minutes. Cut into ½-inch pieces. Set aside.

In 3-quart casserole, combine 3 cups hot water, the rice, bouillon granules and saffron. Cover. Microwave at High for 5 minutes. Microwave at 50% (Medium) for 15 to 25 minutes longer, or until rice is tender and liquid is absorbed. Let stand, covered, for 5 minutes.

In 2-quart casserole, combine peas, peppers and ¼ cup water. Cover. Microwave at High for 4 to 6 minutes, or until peas are defrosted and peppers brighten in color. Drain. Add almonds, chicken, vege-tables, olives and onions to rice. Mix well. Spoon rice mixture into prepared mold. Pack lightly. Invert onto lettuce-lined platter. Serve warm.

Per Serving:					
Calories:	319	Fat:	8 g.	Sodium:	389 mg.
Protein:	18 g.	Cholesterol:	32 mg.	Exchanges:	2 starch, 1 lean meat, 3 vegetable, 1 fat
Carbohydrate:	44 g.				

Dilled Chicken Salad Mold

    Vegetable oil
18 fresh dill sprigs, divided
 1 pkg. (7 oz.) uncooked
      macaroni rings
 1 boneless whole chicken
      breast (8 to 10 oz.), skin
      removed
½ cup diagonally sliced carrot
      (⅛-inch slices)
½ cup chopped celery
½ cup frozen peas
¼ cup plus 2 tablespoons
      water, divided
¼ cup mayonnaise or salad
      dressing
¼ cup sour cream
 1 tablespoon Dijon mustard
 1 tablespoon white wine
      vinegar
½ teaspoon salt
¼ teaspoon pepper
 1 envelope (0.25 oz.)
      unflavored gelatin
½ cup seeded chopped
      cucumber
¼ cup sliced green onions
      Leaf lettuce

4 to 6 servings

Brush 6-cup gelatin mold lightly with vegetable oil. Arrange 8 dill sprigs to cover bottom of mold. Set aside. Prepare macaroni rings as directed on package. Rinse and drain. Set aside.

Place chicken breast on microwave roasting rack. Arrange remaining dill sprigs on chicken breast. Cover with wax paper. Microwave at High for 4 to 6 minutes, or until meat is no longer pink and juices run clear, turning over once. Let stand, covered, for 3 minutes. Remove and discard dill sprigs. Cut chicken into ½-inch pieces. Set aside.

In 1-quart casserole, combine carrot, celery, peas and 2 tablespoons water. Cover. Microwave at High

for 4 to 6 minutes, or until carrots are tender, stirring once. Drain. Set aside. In large mixing bowl, combine mayonnaise, sour cream, mustard, vinegar, salt and pepper. Mix well. Set aside.

In 1-cup measure, sprinkle gelatin over remaining ¼ cup water. Let stand for 5 minutes. Microwave at High for 30 seconds to 1¼ minutes, or until gelatin is dissolved, stirring once. Blend into mayonnaise mixture. Add macaroni, chicken, cooked vegetables, cucumber and onions. Mix well. Spoon into prepared mold. Cover with plastic wrap. Chill about 4 hours, or until set. Dip mold into warm water for 30 seconds. Loosen edges and unmold onto lettuce-lined platter.

Per Serving:						
Calories:	305	Fat:	12 g.	Sodium:	366 mg.	
Protein:	18 g.	Cholesterol:	42 mg.	Exchanges:	1½ starch, 1½ lean meat, 1½ vegetable, 1½ fat	
Carbohydrate:	30 g.					

Centerpiece Salads

Early Summer Salad with Chive Vinaigrette

¼ cup white wine vinegar
2 tablespoons snipped fresh chives
1 clove garlic, minced
½ teaspoon salt
¼ teaspoon pepper
¾ cup olive oil
4 oz. fresh sugar snap peas (about 1 cup)
½ cup water, divided
3 new potatoes (2 oz. each), quartered lengthwise

4 oz. fresh asparagus spears
1 slice farmer cheese, ¼ inch thick (about 2 oz.)
1 tablespoon finely snipped fresh dill weed
6 cups torn mixed greens (Belgian endive, Bibb lettuce, leaf lettuce, radichio and spinach)
6 whole radishes with tops
Fresh chive blossoms

6 to 8 servings

In 2-cup measure, combine vinegar, chives, garlic, salt and pepper. Blend in oil with whisk. Set aside.

In 1-quart casserole, place peas and 2 tablespoons water. Cover. Microwave at High for 3 to 5 minutes, or until peas are very hot and color brightens. Rinse with cold water. Drain. Set aside.

In 1-quart casserole, place potatoes and ¼ cup water. Cover. Microwave at High for 4 to 6 minutes, or until potatoes are tender, stirring once. Rinse with cold water. Drain. Set aside.

In 8-inch square baking dish, place asparagus and the remaining 2 tablespoons water. Cover with plastic wrap. Microwave at High for 3 to 4 minutes, or until asparagus is very hot and color brightens. Rinse with cold water. Drain. Set aside.

Using small cookie cutters (about 1½-inch), cut cheese into shapes. Roll in dill to coat. Arrange mixed greens, cooked vegetables, cheese and radishes on 14-inch platter. Garnish with chive blossoms. Serve with vinaigrette.

NOTE: To serve Early Summer Salad as a main dish for four, arrange 8 slices fully cooked ham (1 oz. each) on platter with vegetables.

Per Serving:			
Calories:	240	Cholesterol:	7 mg.
Protein:	4 g.	Sodium:	181 mg.
Carbohydrate:	8 g.	Exchanges:	½ starch, ½ lean meat, 4 fat
Fat:	22 g.		

Midsummer Fruit Salad with Orange Cream Dressing

½ cup sugar, divided
1 tablespoon cornstarch
½ cup water
1 egg
¼ cup orange juice
  concentrate, defrosted
½ cup whipping cream
4 cups leaf lettuce, torn into
  bite-size pieces
2 cups fresh cherries
2 cups seeded watermelon
  cubes (1-inch cubes)
6 slices cantaloupe
6 slices honeydew melon
2 peaches, sliced (12
  slices each)
10 small clusters seedless green
  and red grapes
½ cup fresh blueberries
½ cup fresh raspberries
2 kiwifruit, peeled, cut in half
  lengthwise and sliced
  (¼-inch slices)
  Fresh mint leaves

  10 to 12 servings

In small mixing bowl, combine ¼ cup sugar and the cornstarch. Blend in water. Microwave at High for 2 to 3 minutes, or until mixture is thickened and translucent, stirring once or twice. Set aside.

Place remaining ¼ cup sugar in 1-cup measure. Blend in egg and concentrate. Microwave at 50% (Medium) for 30 seconds to 2 minutes, or until mixture is slightly thickened, stirring every 30 seconds. Stir small amount of cornstarch mixture gradually into egg mixture. Blend egg mixture back into cornstarch mixture. Chill about 1½ hours, or until cold.

In small mixing bowl, beat whipping cream at high speed of electric mixer until soft peaks form. Fold whipped cream into chilled cornstarch mixture. Set aside.

Arrange lettuce and fruit on 14-inch round platter. Garnish with fresh mint leaves. Serve with dressing.

NOTE: To serve Midsummer Fruit Salad as a dessert, spoon salad and dressing over pound cake or angel food cake slices.

Per Serving:			
Calories:	165	Cholesterol:	37 mg.
Protein:	2 g.	Sodium:	18 mg.
Carbohydrate:	31 g.	Exchanges:	2 fruit, 1 fat
Fat:	5 g.		

Late Summer Marinated Vegetable Salad

2 tablespoons red wine vinegar
1 tablespoon each snipped
   fresh oregano, parsley and
   thyme leaves
1 clove garlic, minced
½ teaspoon dry mustard
¼ teaspoon salt
¼ teaspoon pepper
⅓ cup olive oil
1 cup each fresh cauliflower
   and broccoli flowerets
1 cup sliced carrots
   (¼-inch slices)
¼ cup plus 2 tablespoons
   water, divided
½ cup each green, yellow and
   red pepper strips (3 × ½-inch
   strips)
½ cup each zucchini and yellow
   summer squash slices
   (¼-inch slices)
1 cup halved cherry tomatoes
4 cups leaf lettuce, torn into
   bite-size pieces

10 to 12 servings

In 2-cup measure, combine vinegar, oregano, parsley, thyme, garlic, mustard, salt and pepper. Blend in oil with whisk. Set aside. In 3-quart casserole, combine cauliflower, broccoli, carrots and 2 tablespoons water. Cover. Microwave at High for 5 to 7 minutes, or until vegetables are very hot and colors brighten. Rinse with cold water. Drain. Return to casserole. Set aside.

In medium mixing bowl, combine peppers and 2 tablespoons water. Cover with plastic wrap. Microwave at High for 4 to 5 minutes, or until peppers are very hot and colors brighten. Rinse with cold water. Drain. Add to broccoli mixture. Set aside.

In medium mixing bowl, place squash and the remaining 2 tablespoons water. Cover. Microwave at High for 2 to 4 minutes, or until squash is very hot and colors brighten. Rinse with cold water. Drain. Add squash mixture to broccoli mixture. Add the vinaigrette to vegetable mixture. Add tomatoes. Toss gently to combine. Arrange lettuce on 14-inch platter. Spoon vegetables over lettuce.

NOTE: To serve Late Summer Marinated Vegetable Salad as a main dish for four, add 1 cup quartered pepperoni slices and 1 cup cubed Swiss cheese (½-inch cubes) to vegetable mixture.

Per Serving:			
Calories:	75	Cholesterol:	—
Protein:	1 g.	Sodium:	52 mg.
Carbohydrate:	5 g.	Exchanges:	1 vegetable, 1 fat
Fat:	6 g.		

Fruit Salads

◄ Margarita Fruit Salad

2 teaspoons cornstarch
½ cup nonalcoholic margarita drink mixer
1 tablespoon honey
2 cups cubed honeydew melon (¾-inch cubes)
1 medium banana, sliced (¼-inch slices)

1 cup seedless green grapes
2 kiwifruit, peeled, cut in half lengthwise and sliced (¼-inch slices)
1 jar (6 oz.) maraschino cherries, drained and cut in half
4 lime slices

4 servings

Place cornstarch in 1-cup measure. Add margarita drink mixer. Stir to dissolve cornstarch. Add honey. Microwave at High for 2 to 3 minutes, or until mixture is thickened and translucent, stirring twice. Set aside.

In medium mixing bowl, combine melon, banana, grapes, kiwifruit and cherries. Add thickened margarita mixture. Toss to coat. Cover with plastic wrap. Chill 2 hours, or until cold.

Dip rims of four 8-ounce margarita glasses in margarita drink mixer, then in sugar, if desired. Fill each prepared glass with 1 cup of salad. Garnish each serving with lime slice.

Per Serving:			
Calories:	174	Cholesterol:	—
Protein:	2 g.	Sodium:	12 mg.
Carbohydrate:	45 g.	Exchanges:	3 fruit
Fat:	1 g.		

◄ Minted Melon & Pineapple Salad

1 fresh pineapple (about 3½ lbs.)
2 cups cantaloupe melon balls
2 cups honeydew melon balls

⅓ cup apple jelly
1 tablespoon snipped fresh mint leaves

12 servings

Cut pineapple in half lengthwise, leaving leafy portions attached. With thin, flexible knife, loosen and remove fruit, leaving ½-inch shells. Place shells in 13 × 9-inch baking dish. Cover with plastic wrap. Place in refrigerator.

Cut pineapple into 1-inch cubes. Discard core of pineapple. Place cubed pineapple in medium mixing bowl. Add melon balls. Set aside.

In 1-cup measure, combine jelly and mint. Microwave at High for 1 to 2 minutes, or until jelly is melted, stirring once. Add jelly mixture to fruit. Toss to coat. Cover with plastic wrap. Chill at least 1 hour, or until cold. Spoon fruit mixture into pineapple shells.

Per Serving:			
Calories:	70	Cholesterol:	—
Protein:	1 g.	Sodium:	7 mg.
Carbohydrate:	18 g.	Exchanges:	1 fruit
Fat:	—		

Berry Patch Mousse Salad

2 cups fresh blackberries
2 cups fresh blueberries
2 cups fresh raspberries
1 cup hot water
1 pkg. (3 oz.) strawberry gelatin
1 pkg. (10 oz.) frozen sliced strawberries in syrup
2 cups nondairy whipped topping

8 servings

In medium mixing bowl, combine blackberries, blueberries and raspberries. Toss gently to combine. Set aside.

Place water in 2-quart casserole. Cover. Microwave at High for 2 to 3 minutes, or until water begins to boil. Add gelatin. Stir to dissolve. Add frozen strawberries. Stir until strawberries are defrosted.

Place gelatin mixture in refrigerator for 10 to 15 minutes, or until mixture is soft-set. Fold in whipped topping. Place one-third of berry mixture in 2-quart clear glass salad bowl. Spoon half of gelatin mixture over berries. Repeat layers, ending with berries. Cover with plastic wrap. Chill 4 hours, or until set.

Per Serving:	
Calories:	166
Protein:	3 g.
Carbohydrate:	35 g.
Fat:	3 g.
Cholesterol:	2 mg.
Sodium:	50 mg.
Exchanges:	2½ fruit, 1 fat

Fruited Couscous Salad

1½ cups hot water
  2 tablespoons margarine or
      butter
 ½ teaspoon salt
  1 cup uncooked couscous
 ½ cup frozen orange juice
      concentrate, defrosted
 ⅓ cup sugar
 ¼ cup vegetable oil
  2 tablespoons white wine
      vinegar
  1 teaspoon grated orange
      peel
  1 cup fresh blueberries
  1 cup fresh raspberries
  1 cup fresh strawberries,
      hulled and cut in half
  1 fresh peach, cut into chunks
      (½-inch chunks)
  1 fresh plum, cut into chunks
      (½-inch chunks)
 ¼ cup fresh mint leaves

10 to 12 servings

In 2-quart casserole, combine water, margarine and salt. Cover. Microwave at High for 4 to 8 minutes, or until boiling. Stir in couscous. Re-cover. Let stand for 5 minutes. Fluff couscous lightly with fork. Set aside.

In 2-cup measure, combine concentrate, sugar, oil, vinegar and peel. Blend well with whisk. Add half of juice mixture to couscous. Mix well. Cover and chill at least 1 hour, or until cold.

Add remaining half of juice mixture and remaining ingredients to couscous mixture. Toss gently to combine. Line serving bowl with Bibb lettuce, if desired.

Per Serving:	
Calories:	169
Protein:	2 g.
Carbohydrate:	26 g.
Fat:	7 g.
Cholesterol:	—
Sodium:	113 mg.
Exchanges:	½ starch, 1 fruit, 1½ fat

Wilted Spinach & Fruit Salad

4 slices bacon, cut into ¾-inch
   pieces
¼ cup white vinegar
2 teaspoons packed brown
   sugar
¼ teaspoon salt
4 cups torn fresh spinach
   leaves
2 fresh nectarines, cut into
   8 wedges
2 fresh plums, cut into 8 wedges
1 cup bing cherries, pitted and
   cut in half

4 to 6 servings

Place bacon in 3-quart casserole. Cover with paper towel. Microwave at High for 4 to 8 minutes, or until bacon is brown and crisp, stirring once to break apart.

Drain all but 2 tablespoons of bacon drippings. Stir in vinegar, sugar and salt. Add remaining ingredients. Toss to coat. Serve immediately.

Per Serving:			
Calories:	91	Cholesterol:	4 mg.
Protein:	3 g.	Sodium:	181 mg.
Carbohydrate:	15 g.	Exchanges:	1 vegetable, ½ fruit, ½ fat
Fat:	3 g.		

Sandwiches

Side-by-Side Salami Sandwiches

- 4 green pepper rings
- 4 red pepper rings
- ¼ cup plus 2 tablespoons Italian dressing, divided
- 1 loaf (1 lb.) unsliced rye bread or caraway rye bread
- 4 slices (1 oz. each) Provolone cheese, halved
- 4 slices (1 oz. each) salami, smoked turkey or fully cooked ham
- 1 wooden skewer, 12-inch

4 servings

In 2-quart casserole, combine peppers and 2 tablespoons dressing. Cover. Microwave at High for 2 to 3 minutes, or until peppers are very hot and colors brighten, stirring once. Drain. Set aside.

Cut bread vertically into 4 equal pieces. Slice each piece vertically in half to within ½ inch of bottom crust. Brush remaining ¼ cup dressing evenly in each of 4 slits. Insert 1 green pepper ring, ½ Provolone slice, 1 salami slice, ½ Provolone slice and 1 red pepper ring into each slit.

Thread bread pieces tightly on wooden skewer. Wrap sandwich in paper towels. Microwave at 50% (Medium) for 4 to 5 minutes, or just until warm to the touch and cheese begins to melt, rotating once or twice. Let stand, wrapped, for 5 minutes.

Per Serving:	
Calories:	488
Protein:	22 g.
Carbohydrate:	62 g.
Fat:	18 g.
Cholesterol:	38 mg.
Sodium:	1268 mg.
Exchanges:	3½ starch, 1 high-fat meat, 1 vegetable, 2 fat

Summer Reubens

- 2 plain or cinnamon-raisin bagels, split and toasted Sweet hot mustard
- 4 oz. thin corned beef slices
- 4 thin crosswise slices cored green apple
- 2 oz. Brie cheese, thinly sliced

2 servings

Spread cut sides of each bagel half with mustard. Place each bottom half cut-side-up on paper towel. Top evenly with corned beef, apple and cheese slices. Add bagel tops. Fold corners of paper towel over each sandwich to enclose. Place folded-side-down on plate.

Microwave sandwiches at High for 45 seconds to 1 minute, or just until warm to the touch, rotating and rearranging sandwiches once.

Per Serving:	
Calories:	418
Protein:	23 g.
Carbohydrate:	34 g.
Fat:	21 g.
Cholesterol:	84 mg.
Sodium:	1148 mg.
Exchanges:	2 starch, 2½ high-fat meat

Pickled Kabobs

Wooden skewers, 6-inch
Cherry tomatoes
Marinated artichoke hearts
Pickled cherry peppers
Pickled chili peppers
Pickled baby corn
Spanish olives
Pickled mushrooms
Pickled carrots
Bread-and-butter-pickle chunks
Tiny dill pickles

On each wooden skewer, thread desired items. Serve kabobs with sandwiches.

Because items on kabobs will vary, nutritional information cannot be calculated.

South of the Border Muffuletta

1 loaf (1 lb.) round sourdough bread
¼ cup margarine or butter
1 tablespoon sliced green onion
1 clove garlic, minced
⅛ teaspoon chili powder
⅛ teaspoon ground cumin
6 slices (0.5 oz. each) fully cooked chicken breast
3 slices (1 oz. each) Monterey Jack cheese
1 can (4 oz.) whole green chilies, drained and sliced in half lengthwise
4 slices tomato
Leaf lettuce

6 servings

Cut loaf in half crosswise. Cut circle 1 inch from outer edge of crust. Remove bread from circle to 1-inch depth. Reserve bread for future use. Set halves aside.

In small mixing bowl, microwave margarine at 30% (Medium Low) for 15 to 30 seconds, or until soft-ened. Add onion, garlic, chili pow-der and cumin. Mix well. Spread margarine mixture evenly over inside of top and bottom of loaf.

Layer 2 chicken breast slices, 1 cheese slice, half of chilies, 2 tomato slices and lettuce. Repeat layers once. Top with 2 chicken breast slices and 1 cheese slice. Place top of loaf over filling. Serve in wedges.

Per Serving:	
Calories:	370
Protein:	15 g.
Carbohydrate:	44 g.
Fat:	15 g.
Cholesterol:	27 mg.
Sodium:	785 mg.
Exchanges:	2½ starch, ½ lean meat, 1 vegetable, 2½ fat

Salami & Cheese Muffuletta

1 loaf (1 lb.) round sourdough bread
¼ cup snipped fresh basil leaves
¼ cup olive or vegetable oil
1 clove garlic, minced
Fresh spinach leaves
3 slices (1 oz. each) Colby cheese
9 slices (0.5 oz. each) salami, rolled
2 slices (1 oz. each) Provolone cheese
4 slices Roma tomato

6 servings

Cut loaf in half crosswise. Cut circle 1 inch from outer edge of crust. Remove bread from circle to 1-inch depth. Reserve bread for future use. Set halves aside.

In 1-cup measure, combine basil, oil and garlic. Brush mixture evenly over inside of top and bottom of loaf. Arrange spinach leaves evenly over bottom half of loaf.

Layer 1 slice Colby, 3 slices salami, 1 slice Provolone, 3 slices salami, 1 slice Colby, the tomato slices, 1 slice Provolone, 3 slices salami and 1 slice Colby. Top evenly with spinach leaves. Place top of loaf over filling.

Wrap loaf in paper towels. Microwave at 50% (Medium) for 4 to 6 minutes, or just until warm to the touch and cheese begins to melt, rotating once or twice. Let stand, wrapped, for 5 minutes. Serve in wedges.

Per Serving:	
Calories:	446
Protein:	16 g.
Carbohydrate:	44 g.
Fat:	23 g.
Cholesterol:	35 mg.
Sodium:	861 mg.
Exchanges:	2½ starch, 1 high-fat meat, 1 vegetable, 3 fat

Steamed Lettuce Leaves

Large outer leaves from head
    of lettuce

1 or 2 servings

Wrap 1 or 2 leaves between 2
dampened paper towels. Microwave at High for 15 to 30 seconds,
or until warm but still crisp. Place
¼ to ½ cup desired filling (opposite) on each leaf. Fold up to enclose filling.

Per Serving:
Calories: 1
Protein: —
Carbohydrate: —
Fat: —
Cholesterol: —
Sodium: 1 mg.
Exchanges: free

Cold Barbecue Turkey Filling

1 cup frozen peas
2 tablespoons water
½ lb. fully cooked turkey, cut into thin strips (2 × ¼-inch strips)
½ cup shredded carrot
¼ cup mayonnaise or salad dressing
1 tablespoon barbecue sauce

4 servings

In 1-quart casserole, combine peas and water. Cover. Microwave at High for 2 to 3 minutes, or until peas are defrosted. Rinse with cold water. Drain.

In medium mixing bowl, combine peas, turkey and carrot. Set aside. In small bowl, combine mayonnaise and barbecue sauce. Mix well. Add to turkey mixture. Toss to coat. Cover with plastic wrap.

Chill about 2 hours, or until cold. Serve in Steamed Lettuce Leaves (opposite) or as sandwich filling.

Per Serving:			
Calories:	256	Cholesterol:	61 mg.
Protein:	23 g.	Sodium:	206 mg.
Carbohydrate:	7 g.	Exchanges:	½ starch, 3 lean meat, 1 fat
Fat:	15 g.		

Crunchy Tuna Filling

1 tablespoon margarine or butter
¼ cup slivered almonds
2 cups cored and chopped Granny Smith or Rome apple (8 oz. apple)
1 can (6½ oz.) solid white tuna, water pack, drained and flaked
½ cup shredded Cheddar cheese
¼ cup mayonnaise or salad dressing
1 teaspoon lemon juice
⅛ teaspoon salt

4 servings

In 9-inch pie plate, microwave margarine at High for 45 seconds to 1 minute, or until melted. Stir in almonds. Toss to coat. Microwave at High for 3½ to 4½ minutes, or until light golden brown, stirring every 2 minutes. Let stand for 5 minutes.

In medium mixing bowl, combine toasted almonds and remaining ingredients. Mix well. Cover with plastic wrap.

Chill about 2 hours, or until cold. Serve in Steamed Lettuce Leaves (opposite) or as sandwich filling.

Per Serving:			
Calories:	327	Cholesterol:	52 mg.
Protein:	18 g.	Sodium:	668 mg.
Carbohydrate:	12 g.	Exchanges:	2½ lean meat, 1 fruit, 3 fat
Fat:	24 g.		

Cucumber Shrimp Filling

Salad:
1 pkg. (10 oz.) frozen cooked medium shrimp, shelled and deveined, defrosted
1 medium cucumber, peeled, seeded and chopped (about 1¾ cups)
⅓ cup seeded chopped tomato
¼ cup sliced green onions

Dressing:
2 tablespoons vegetable oil
1 tablespoon lime juice
½ teaspoon ground cumin
¼ teaspoon garlic salt
⅛ teaspoon cayenne

4 servings

In medium mixing bowl, combine all salad ingredients. Set aside. In small bowl, combine all dressing ingredients. Set aside. Mix well. Add to salad. Toss to coat. Cover with plastic wrap.

Chill about 2 hours, or until cold. Serve in Steamed Lettuce Leaves (opposite) or as sandwich filling.

Per Serving:			
Calories:	145	Cholesterol:	138 mg.
Protein:	16 g.	Sodium:	278 mg.
Carbohydrate:	3 g.	Exchanges:	2 lean meat, ½ vegetable, ½ fat
Fat:	8 g.		

Roast Beef & Avocado Rolls ▲

- 4 lahvosh crackerbread rounds (5-inch)
- 1 avocado (6 to 8 oz.)
- ¼ cup sliced green onions
- 1 teaspoon lemon juice
- 1 clove garlic, minced
- ⅛ teaspoon salt
- 4 thin slices fully cooked roast beef (1 oz. each)
- ½ cup alfalfa sprouts

4 servings

Per Serving:	
Calories:	214
Protein:	11 g.
Carbohydrate:	17 g.
Fat:	12 g.
Cholesterol:	20 mg.
Sodium:	278 mg.
Exchanges:	1 starch, 1 lean meat, ½ vegetable, 1½ fat

How to Microwave Roast Beef & Avocado Rolls

Wet both sides of each lahvosh round by holding briefly under cold running water. Place each wet round between 2 dampened paper towels. Stack rounds and place on plate.

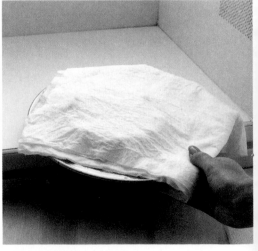

Microwave at High for 1 to 3 minutes, or just until warm to the touch. Let stand for 5 minutes to soften.

Inside-out Pizza Sandwiches

Italian Bread:

1 loaf (1 lb.) frozen white bread dough*
  Softened margarine or butter
  Olive oil
1 large clove garlic, minced
1 teaspoon Italian seasoning

Filling:

1 small green pepper, cut in half lengthwise, thinly sliced
1 tablespoon olive oil
2 cups shredded mozzarella cheese (8 oz.)
2 oz. sliced pepperoni
½ cup seeded chopped tomato

8 servings

Per Serving:	
Calories:	310
Protein:	14 g.
Carbohydrate:	29 g.
Fat:	15 g.
Cholesterol:	24 mg.
Sodium:	585 mg.
Exchanges:	2 starch,
	1 high-fat meat, 1 fat

Rub dough on all sides with softened margarine. Roll up in sheet of wax paper. Twist ends to seal. Place loaf in microwave oven. Microwave at 50% (Medium) for 2 minutes, rotating loaf once. Let stand for 5 minutes.

Turn loaf over. Microwave at 50% (Medium) for 1 to 2 minutes, or until dough is soft to the touch and slightly warm. Let stand to complete defrosting. Brush large baking sheet with oil. Set aside.

Shape dough into 8-inch circle. Place on prepared baking sheet. Cover with cloth and let rise in warm place about 45 minutes to 1½ hours, or until doubled in size.

Preheat conventional oven to 400°F. Using fingertips, make indentations randomly over surface of dough. Brush lightly with oil. In small bowl, mix garlic and Italian seasoning. Sprinkle over top of dough. Bake for 15 to 23 minutes, or until golden brown. Let cool completely.

In 1-quart casserole, combine green pepper and 1 tablespoon oil. Cover. Microwave at High for 3 to 6 minutes, or until tender, stirring once or twice. Drain.

Slice loaf in half horizontally. Place bottom half of loaf cut-side-up on paper-towel-lined plate. Sprinkle with 1 cup shredded mozzarella. Top evenly with pepperoni, green pepper and chopped tomato. Top with remaining 1 cup mozzarella and top of loaf. Microwave at 50% (Medium) for 3 to 4 minutes, or until loaf is warm and cheese begins to melt. Let stand for 2 minutes. Serve in wedges.

*If desired, substitute 1 lb. baked Focaccia loaf (found in Italian delis and bakeries) for Italian bread.

Remove peel and pit from avocado. Cut avocado into chunks. Mash with fork in small mixing bowl. Add onions, lemon juice, garlic and salt. Mix well.

Spread one-fourth of avocado mixture evenly on each softened lahvosh round. Top each with 1 slice roast beef and 2 tablespoons sprouts.

Roll up to enclose filling. Secure with wooden pick. Serve immediately, or chill up to 2 hours.

Toasted Nut & Ham Loaf ▲

- 1 loaf (1 lb.) whole wheat or white French bread
- 2 tablespoons margarine or butter
- ½ cup chopped pecans
- 1 lb. ground fully cooked ham
- 1 large carrot, grated (about ¾ cup)
- ½ cup finely chopped green pepper
- ¼ cup finely chopped onion
- ¾ cup mayonnaise or salad dressing
- 1 tablespoon prepared horseradish

8 to 10 servings

Per Serving:	
Calories:	364
Protein:	15 g.
Carbohydrate:	26 g.
Fat:	24 g.
Cholesterol:	35 mg.
Sodium:	912 mg.
Exchanges:	1½ starch, 1 lean meat, 1 vegetable, 4 fat

How to Microwave Toasted Nut & Ham Loaf

Trim ends from French bread. Cut loaf in half vertically. Using long, serrated knife, remove bread from center of each loaf half, leaving ¼-inch shell. Reserve bread for future use. Set halves aside.

Microwave margarine in 9-inch pie plate at High for 45 seconds to 1 minute, or until melted. Add pecans. Toss to coat. Microwave at High for 5 to 8½ minutes, or until toasted, stirring after every minute. Drain on paper towels. Set aside.

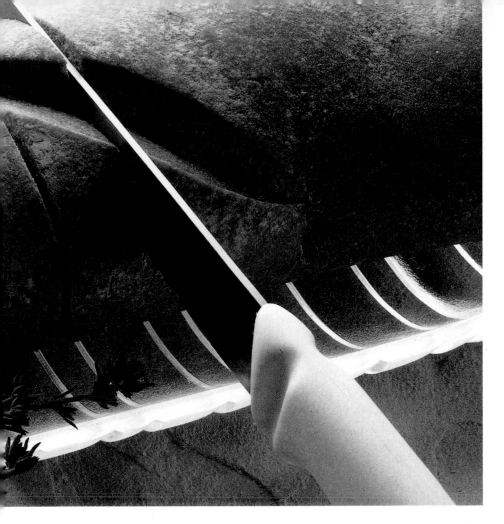

Herbed Breast of Chicken Sandwiches

2 boneless whole chicken breasts (8 to 10 oz. each), skin removed, split in half
2 tablespoons olive oil
1 tablespoon white wine vinegar
1 tablespoon fresh thyme leaves
1 teaspoon grated lemon peel
¼ teaspoon salt
⅛ teaspoon pepper
4 French rolls (6 to 8-inch) or hamburger buns
 Mayonnaise
 Watercress or Bibb lettuce
 Tomato slices
 Onion slices

4 servings

In 9-inch round cake dish, arrange chicken breast halves with meaty portions toward outside. Set aside.

In small bowl, combine oil, vinegar, thyme, lemon peel, salt and pepper. Spoon mixture over chicken breasts. Cover with plastic wrap. Let stand at room temperature for 10 minutes.

Microwave at High for 5 to 6 minutes, or until chicken is no longer pink and juices run clear, rotating dish and rearranging breast halves once. Chill about 6 hours, or until cold. Serve on rolls with mayonnaise, watercress, tomato and onion.

Combine remaining ingredients in large mixing bowl. Mix well. Add toasted pecans. Mix well. Divide mixture in half.

Stuff each bread half with half of filling mixture. Wrap each with plastic wrap. Chill about 2 hours, or until firm. To serve, slice each loaf half into ten 1-inch slices.

Per Serving:	
Calories:	358
Protein:	31 g.
Carbohydrate:	24 g.
Fat:	15 g.
Cholesterol:	76 mg.
Sodium:	453 mg.
Exchanges:	1½ starch,
	3½ lean meat,
	½ vegetable, 1 fat

Micro-grilling

Barbecue Techniques

America's favorite summer ritual centers around the outdoor grill. It looks easy enough, but a successful barbecue demands more than lighting a fire and putting meat on the grill. Everyone knows the backyard chef who serves up barbecued chicken burnt on the outside and raw in the center.

Combining the microwave oven with a charcoal or gas grill offers several advantages. It reduces cooking time, especially for smaller items like chicken pieces and ribs. It prevents drying of foods like pork chops and turkey burgers, which need to reach high internal temperatures. And, partial cooking by microwave ensures that meats will be

succulent and fully cooked inside by the time the grill gives them a rich, golden brown color and the distinctive aroma and flavor of barbecued meat.

For perfect results and food safety, follow recipe directions carefully.

The grill and the pre-microwaved foods should be ready at the same time. Take food directly from the microwave oven to the grill. Wind and weather affect cooking times, so use recipe times as guidelines and check food for doneness periodically, as directed.

Prepare the Grill First

If you are charcoal-grilling pork chops or poultry pieces directly over medium-hot to medium coals, start the charcoal first. Wait until coals are barely covered with gray ash and temperature tests hot at grill level before pre-microwaving meat.

When charcoal-grilling large cuts, such as a whole turkey, use the indirect method, with hot coals banked to one side of a drip pan. Light charcoal, wait about twenty minutes, then pre-microwave meat while the fire reaches hot temperature.

With a gas grill that preheats in ten minutes, turn on the grill, then pre-microwave meat. When using the indirect method with a two-burner grill, preheat both sides, then turn off burner under drip pan and meat.

How to Arrange Fire

Direct Heat. Spread a single layer of coals or lava rocks under food and 1 inch beyond. Stack coals in pyramid to light fire; when a light covering of ash forms, spread coals out again.

Indirect Charcoal Heat. Place aluminum foil drip pan on one side of grate. Heap coals beside it. When fire is hot, arrange food on cooking grid directly over drip pan. To maintain temperature, add a few more coals every 30 to 45 minutes. **Indirect Gas Heat.** Remove cooking grid. Preheat grill on high setting for 10 minutes. Place foil drip pan on lava rocks on one side of grate. (With two-burner grill, turn off burner under drip pan.) Replace grid and arrange food over drip pan.

Two Ways to Judge Fire Temperature

Appearance. Once coals develop light, uniform covering of gray ash, fire is HOT.

A heavier layer of ash reduces temperature to MEDIUM. Coals glow through ash.

A thick layer of ash insulates coals and reduces temperature to LOW.

Heat. Check temperature by cautiously extending palm of hand over coals at cooking level. Count the seconds hand can be held over coals: 2 seconds, HOT; 3 seconds, MEDIUM-HOT; 4 seconds, MEDIUM; 5 seconds, LOW.

Three Ways to Control Heat

Adjust grid height. Raise grid to slow cooking for longer-cooking items, such as chicken breasts and ribs. Lower grid height when you need more heat for fast-cooking items, such as chicken wings, fully cooked brats and hot dogs.

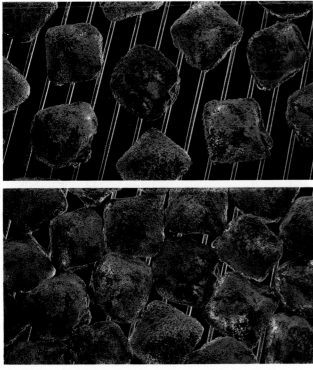

Adjust coals. Spread coals out to reduce fire temperature. Increase heat by moving coals closer together and tapping off ash. With gas grill, turn temperature up or down. Use a higher setting on cold or windy days.

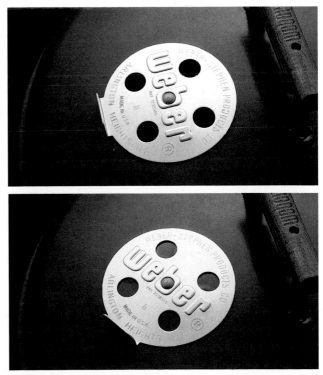

Adjust vent holes. On covered grill, open vents to allow more air flow, which increases temperature. Partially close vents to reduce heat. Fully closed vents will smother coals.

Micro-grill Meat Chart

Micro-grilling takes the guesswork out of barbecuing poultry and pork. These meats must reach a high internal temperature in order to be fully cooked. With grilling alone, they can burn on the surface before the interior is done. Beef and lamb are not included in this chart because they can be served at lower internal temperatures.

Item	Weight	Microwave Start	Grill Finish
Poultry			
Chicken Wings (about 10 wings)	2 lbs.	Cut each wing into 3 pieces, separating at joints. Discard tips. Arrange pieces in 10-inch square casserole. Cover with wax paper. Microwave at High for 9 to 16 minutes, or until exterior is no longer pink, stirring twice.	Place on cooking grid over medium direct heat. Grill, uncovered, for about 10 minutes, or until meat is no longer pink and juices run clear, basting with desired sauce and turning frequently.
Chicken Breasts, bone-in or boneless (4 halves)	8 to 10 oz. each	Remove skin, if desired. Arrange breast halves in 9-inch round cake dish with meaty portions toward outside edges. Cover with wax paper. Microwave at High for 4 to 6 minutes, or until exterior is no longer pink, rearranging twice.	Place on cooking grid over low direct heat. Grill, uncovered, for 8 to 12 minutes, or until meat is no longer pink and juices run clear, basting with desired sauce and turning once.
Whole Chicken	2½ to 3 lbs.	Remove giblets. Rinse with cold water. Place breast-side-down in 10-inch square casserole. Cover with wax paper. Microwave at High for 10 minutes, turning breast-side-up after half the time.	Place on cooking grid over high indirect heat. Grill, covered, for 40 to 45 minutes, or until internal temperature in meaty portions of both thighs registers 185°F and juices run clear, rotating chicken once. Let stand, tented with foil, for 10 minutes before carving.
Chicken Pieces	2½ to 3 lbs.	Arrange pieces in 10-inch square casserole with meaty portions toward outside edges. Cover with wax paper. Microwave at High for 13 to 15 minutes, or until exterior is no longer pink, rearranging twice.	Place on cooking grid over low direct heat. Grill, covered, for 20 to 35 minutes, or until meat is no longer pink and juices run clear, basting with desired sauce or melted butter and turning pieces twice.
Whole Turkey	6 to 8 lbs.	Remove giblets. Rinse with cold water. Place breast-side-down in 10-inch square casserole. Microwave at High for 10 minutes. Microwave at 50% (Medium) for 50 minutes longer, or until exterior is no longer pink, turning over after half the time.	Place on cooking grid over medium indirect heat. Grill, covered, for 1 hour 10 minutes to 1 hour 40 minutes, or until internal temperature in meaty portions of thighs registers 185°F, rotating turkey once. Let stand, tented with foil, for 10 minutes before carving.
Turkey Breast, bone-in	5 to 6 lbs.	Place breast-side-down in 10-inch square casserole. Cover with wax paper. Microwave at High for 5 minutes. Microwave at 70% (Medium High) for 20 minutes longer, turning breast-side-up after half the time.	Place on cooking grid over medium indirect heat. Grill, covered, for 55 minutes to 1 hour 15 minutes, or until internal temperature registers 175°F in both breast halves, rotating breast once. Let stand, tented with foil, for 10 minutes before carving.
Turkey Tenderloins (2 tenderloins)	12 oz. each	Arrange tenderloins in 8-inch square baking dish. Cover with wax paper. Microwave at 70% (Medium High) for 5 to 6 minutes, or until edges are no longer pink, turning over once.	Place on cooking grid over medium direct heat. Grill, covered, for 10 to 14 minutes, or until meat is no longer pink and internal temperature registers 175°F, turning once.

Item	Weight	Microwave Start	Grill Finish
Turkey Drumsticks (4 drumsticks)	12 oz. each	Arrange on microwave roasting rack. Cover with wax paper. Microwave at 70% (Medium High) for 15 to 20 minutes, or until exterior is no longer pink, turning over and re-arranging once.	Place on cooking grid over low direct heat. Grill, covered, for 25 to 30 minutes, or until internal temperature registers 185°F, basting with desired sauce or melted butter and turning frequently. Let stand, tented with foil, for 10 minutes.
Cornish Game Hens (4 game hens)	18 oz. each	Remove giblets. Rinse with cold water. Secure legs with string. Place breast-side-down in 10-inch square casserole. Cover with wax paper. Microwave at High for 10 to 15 minutes, turning breast-side-up after half the time.	Place on cooking grid over medium indirect heat. Grill, covered, for 40 to 45 minutes, or until internal temperature in meaty portion of thighs registers 185°F and juices run clear, rotating hens once. Let stand, tented with foil, for 10 minutes.
Pork			
Spare Ribs	3 lbs.	Cut ribs into serving-size portions. Place 1 tbsp. flour in oven cooking bag. Hold bag closed. Shake to coat. Add ribs, ½ cup each chopped green pepper and chopped onion and ¼ cup water to bag. Secure bag with nylon tie. Place in 10-inch square casserole. Make six ½-inch slits in neck of bag below tie. Microwave at High for 5 minutes. Microwave at 50% (Medium) for 20 to 25 minutes longer, or until tender, turning bag over once. Let bag stand, closed, for 10 minutes. Remove ribs from bag.	Place on cooking grid over low direct heat. Grill, covered, for 10 to 12 minutes, or until deep golden brown, basting with desired sauce and turning several times.
Country-style Ribs	3 lbs.	Cut ribs into serving-size portions. Follow method for Spare Ribs (above), except microwave at 50% (Medium) for 30 to 35 minutes, or until tender, turning bag over once. Let bag stand, closed, for 10 minutes. Remove ribs from bag.	Place on cooking grid over low direct heat. Grill, covered, for 10 to 12 minutes, or until deep golden brown, basting with desired sauce and turning several times.
Pork Chops (about 4 chops)	4 oz. each	Arrange chops on microwave roasting rack with meaty portions toward outside. Cover with wax paper. Microwave at 70% (Medium High) for 8 to 10 minutes, or until edges are no longer pink, turning over once.	Place on cooking grid over low direct heat. Grill, covered, for 7 to 12 minutes, or until meat near bone is no longer pink, turning once.
Fresh Bratwurst (about 6)	1½ lbs.	Arrange brats in single layer in 8-inch square baking dish. Add ½ cup water. Cover with plastic wrap. Microwave at High for 8 to 11 minutes, or until firm and no longer pink, rearranging once. Drain.	Place on cooking grid over medium direct heat. Grill, uncovered, for 5 to 8 minutes, or until golden brown, turning frequently.

Sauces, Marinades & Butters

Traditional Barbecue Sauce

½ cup chopped onion
2 tablespoons vegetable oil
2 cloves garlic, minced
1 can (14½ oz.) Italian plum tomatoes, cut up and undrained
¾ cup cola-flavored soda
1 can (6 oz.) tomato paste
⅓ cup catsup
2 tablespoons packed brown sugar
2 tablespoons Worcestershire sauce
2 tablespoons cider vinegar
¼ teaspoon red pepper sauce
¼ teaspoon celery seed

4 cups
16 servings

In 2-quart casserole, combine onion, oil and garlic. Cover. Microwave at High for 2 to 3 minutes, or until onion is tender, stirring once.

Add remaining ingredients. Mix well. Cover with wax paper. Microwave at High for 5 minutes. Stir. Re-cover. Microwave at 50% (Medium) for 15 to 20 minutes, or until sauce is thickened and flavors are blended, stirring once or twice.

Store, covered, in refrigerator up to 2 weeks. Brush chicken, turkey, beef or pork with sauce during last minutes of grilling, turning several times. Serve with additional sauce, if desired.

Per Serving:	
Calories:	50
Protein:	1 g.
Carbohydrate:	8 g.
Fat:	2 g.
Cholesterol:	—
Sodium:	207 mg.
Exchanges:	1½ vegetable, ½ fat

Jamaican Hot & Spicy Barbecue Sauce

1 cup chopped onion
¼ cup dark rum
¼ cup packed brown sugar
2 cloves garlic, finely chopped
1 can (15 oz.) tomato sauce
½ cup catsup
1 tablespoon prepared mustard
¼ to ½ teaspoon cayenne
¼ teaspoon ground cinnamon

2½ cups
10 servings

In 2-quart casserole, combine onion, rum, sugar and garlic. Mix well. Cover. Microwave at High for 5 to 6 minutes, or until onion is tender, stirring once or twice.

Add remaining ingredients. Mix well. Cover with wax paper. Microwave at High for 5 minutes. Stir. Re-cover. Microwave at 50% (Medium) for 10 to 15 minutes, or until sauce is thickened and flavors are blended, stirring once or twice.

Store, covered, in refrigerator up to 2 weeks. Brush chicken, turkey, beef or pork with sauce during last minutes of grilling, turning several times. Serve with additional sauce, if desired.

Per Serving:	
Calories:	69
Protein:	1 g.
Carbohydrate:	13 g.
Fat:	—
Cholesterol:	—
Sodium:	420 mg.
Exchanges:	2½ vegetable

Hickory Smoke Barbecue Sauce

½ cup chopped onion
2 tablespoons vegetable oil
2 cloves garlic, minced
1 can (15 oz.) tomato sauce
⅔ cup chili sauce
3 tablespoons frozen orange juice concentrate
2 tablespoons packed brown sugar
1 teaspoon liquid smoke flavoring

2 cups
8 servings

In 2-quart casserole, combine onion, oil and garlic. Cover. Microwave at High for 2 to 3 minutes, or until onion is tender, stirring once.

Add remaining ingredients. Mix well. Cover with wax paper. Microwave at High for 5 minutes. Stir. Re-cover. Microwave at 50% (Medium) for 10 to 15 minutes, or until sauce is thickened and flavors are blended, stirring once or twice.

Store, covered, in refrigerator up to 2 weeks. Brush chicken, turkey, beef or pork with sauce during last minutes of grilling, turning several times. Serve with additional sauce, if desired.

Per Serving:	
Calories:	97
Protein:	2 g.
Carbohydrate:	16 g.
Fat:	4 g.
Cholesterol:	—
Sodium:	628 mg.
Exchanges:	3 vegetable, ½ fat

Pictured clockwise from bottom: Oriental Marinade (page 79); Traditional Barbecue Sauce (above); Tequila Marinade (page 78)

Tequila Marinade

1 can (6 oz.) frozen limeade
  concentrate
½ cup vegetable oil
⅓ cup tequila
¼ cup red wine vinegar

2 cloves garlic, minced
½ teaspoon chili powder
½ teaspoon ground cumin
¼ teaspoon salt
⅛ teaspoon pepper

2 cups
16 servings

In 4-cup measure, place frozen concentrate. Microwave at High for 1 to 2½ minutes, or until defrosted, stirring once. Add remaining ingredients. Blend well with whisk. Store marinade, covered, in refrigerator up to 2 weeks.

Place chicken, turkey, beef or pork in large plastic food-storage bag. Add 1 cup marinade. Secure bag. Chill at least 2 hours or overnight, turning bag occasionally. Drain and discard marinade. Micro-grill meat as directed in chart (pages 74 and 75).

Per Serving:			
Calories:	25	Cholesterol:	—
Protein:	—	Sodium:	8 mg.
Carbohydrate:	2 g.	Exchanges:	½ fat
Fat:	2 g.		

Tangy Beer Marinade

1 cup beer
¼ cup vegetable oil
2 tablespoons Dijon mustard
2 teaspoons sugar
¼ teaspoon salt
¼ teaspoon pepper

1¼ cups
10 servings

In 2-cup measure, combine all ingredients. Blend with whisk. Store marinade, covered, in refrigerator up to 1 week.

Place chicken, turkey or pork in large plastic food-storage bag. Add marinade. Secure bag. Chill at least 2 hours or overnight, turning bag occasionally. Drain and discard marinade. Micro-grill meat as directed in chart (pages 74 and 75).

Per Serving:
Calories: 16
Protein: —
Carbohydrate: —
Fat: 1 g.
Cholesterol: —
Sodium: 34 mg.
Exchanges: free

Oriental Marinade

½ cup chopped onion
1 tablespoon sesame oil
1 tablespoon vegetable oil
1 tablespoon minced fresh gingerroot
2 cloves garlic, minced
1½ cups plum preserves
2 tablespoons hoisin sauce
1 tablespoon soy sauce

2 cups
16 servings

In 2-quart casserole, combine onion, oils, gingerroot and garlic. Cover. Microwave at High for 2 to 3 minutes, or until onion is tender, stirring once.

Add preserves, hoisin sauce and soy sauce. Microwave at High for 2 to 4 minutes, or until preserves can be stirred smooth, stirring once or twice. Store marinade, covered, in refrigerator up to 1 week.

Place chicken, turkey, beef or pork in large plastic food-storage bag. Add 1 cup marinade. Secure bag. Chill 2 to 4 hours, turning bag occasionally. Drain and discard marinade. Micro-grill meat as directed in chart (pages 74 and 75). Brush meat with remaining marinade during last minutes of grilling, if desired, turning several times.

Per Serving:
Calories: 24
Protein: —
Carbohydrate: 5 g.
Fat: —
Cholesterol: —
Sodium: 21 mg.
Exchanges: ½ fruit

Herb & Blue Cheese Marinade

1 cup vegetable oil, divided
2 tablespoons chopped onion
2 cloves garlic, minced
¼ cup white vinegar
1 teaspoon dried basil leaves
1 teaspoon dry mustard
1 teaspoon sugar
1 teaspoon salt
¼ teaspoon pepper
¼ teaspoon crushed red pepper flakes
¼ cup crumbled blue cheese

1½ cups
12 servings

In 1-quart casserole, combine 2 tablespoons oil, the onion and garlic. Cover. Microwave at High for 2 to 3 minutes, or until onion is tender, stirring once.

Add remaining ¾ cup plus 2 tablespoons oil and remaining ingredients, except blue cheese. Blend with whisk. Stir in blue cheese. Store marinade, covered, in refrigerator up to 1 week.

Place chicken, turkey, beef or pork in large plastic food-storage bag. Add marinade. Secure bag. Chill at least 2 hours or overnight, turning bag occasionally. Drain and discard marinade. Micro-grill meat as directed in chart (pages 74 and 75).

Per Serving:
Calories: 44
Protein: —
Carbohydrate: —
Fat: 5 g.
Cholesterol: 1 mg.
Sodium: 54 mg.
Exchanges: 1 fat

Peach Cayenne Butter ◄

1 small peach, peeled and cut
   into chunks (about 4 to 6 oz.)
½ cup butter or margarine
⅛ teaspoon cayenne
⅛ teaspoon ground cinnamon

½ cup
8 servings

In food processor or blender, process peach until finely chopped. In small mixing bowl, microwave butter at 30% (Medium Low) for 15 seconds to 1 minute, or until softened, checking every 15 seconds.

Add butter, cayenne and cinnamon to peach in processor. Process until mixture is smooth.

Store, covered, in refrigerator up to 2 weeks. Brush chicken, turkey, beef or pork with butter during last minutes of grilling.

Per Serving:	
Calories:	107
Protein:	—
Carbohydrate:	1 g.
Fat:	12 g.
Cholesterol:	31 mg.
Sodium:	117 mg.
Exchanges:	2 fat

◄ Honey-Mustard Sauce

¼ cup chopped onion	¼ cup prepared mustard
1 tablespoon vegetable oil	2 tablespoons fresh lemon
2 teaspoons mustard seed	juice
⅓ cup honey	

¾ cup
6 servings

In 1-quart casserole, combine onion, oil and mustard seed. Cover. Microwave at High for 2 to 3 minutes, or until onion is very tender, stirring once.

Add remaining ingredients, stirring with whisk until combined. Microwave at High, uncovered, for 1½ to 3½ minutes, or until mixture is very hot and begins to boil, stirring once.

Store, covered, in refrigerator up to 2 weeks. Brush chicken, fish or pork with sauce during last minutes of grilling, turning several times. Serve with additional sauce, if desired.

Per Serving:			
Calories:	93	Cholesterol:	—
Protein:	1 g.	Sodium:	126 mg.
Carbohydrate:	17 g.	Exchanges:	½ vegetable, 1 fruit, ½ fat
Fat:	3 g.		

◄ Jalapeño Butter

½ cup butter or margarine	½ teaspoon grated lime peel
2 tablespoons canned sliced jalapeño peppers, drained and chopped	⅛ teaspoon ground cumin

½ cup
8 servings

In small mixing bowl, microwave butter at 30% (Medium Low) for 15 seconds to 1 minute, or until softened, checking every 15 seconds. Stir in remaining ingredients.

Store, covered, in refrigerator up to 2 weeks. Brush chicken, turkey, beef or pork with butter during last minutes of grilling, turning several times.

Chili Butter: Follow recipe above, except substitute 2 tablespoons canned chopped green chilies, drained, for jalapeño peppers.

Herb Butter: Follow recipe above, except substitute 2 teaspoons snipped fresh basil leaves, 2 teaspoons snipped fresh oregano leaves and 2 teaspoons snipped fresh thyme leaves for jalapeño peppers, lime peel and cumin.

Per Serving:			
Calories:	103	Cholesterol:	31 mg.
Protein:	—	Sodium:	117 mg.
Carbohydrate:	—	Exchanges:	2 fat
Fat:	12 g.		

Raspberry Catsup

2 cups fresh raspberries	
½ cup chopped onion	
1 tablespoon vegetable oil	
2 cloves garlic, minced	
1 can (15 oz.) tomato sauce	
¼ cup tomato paste	
3 tablespoons packed brown sugar	
2 tablespoons white vinegar	
½ teaspoon salt	

2 cups
8 servings

In 2-quart casserole, combine raspberries, onion, oil and garlic. Cover. Microwave at High for 7 to 8 minutes, or until onion is tender, stirring 2 or 3 times.

Add remaining ingredients. Mix well. Cover with wax paper. Microwave at High for 5 minutes. Stir. Re-cover. Microwave at 50% (Medium) for 10 to 12 minutes, or until sauce is slightly thickened, stirring once or twice. Cool slightly.

Strain mixture through wire strainer into 4-cup measure, pressing with back of spoon. Discard pulp.

Cover sauce and chill about 6 hours, or until cold. Store, covered, in refrigerator up to 2 weeks. Serve catsup with chicken, turkey, beef or pork.

Per Serving:	
Calories:	77
Protein:	1 g.
Carbohydrate:	15 g.
Fat:	2 g.
Cholesterol:	—
Sodium:	521 mg.
Exchanges:	1½ vegetable, ½ fruit

Micro-grilled Meats

◀ Smoked Turkey

| 4 cups water | 6 to 8-lb. turkey |
| 2 cups wood smoking chips | |

6 to 8 servings

Place water and wood chips in large mixing bowl. Soak chips for 1 hour. Drain on paper towels. Place in center of 16-inch sheet of heavy-duty foil. Bring short edges of foil together and fold down to make log. Set log aside.

Place turkey breast-side-down in 10-inch square casserole. Microwave at High for 10 minutes. Microwave at 50% (Medium) for 50 minutes longer, or until exterior of turkey is no longer pink, turning turkey breast-side-up after half the cooking time. (Prepare grill for medium indirect heat during last 30 minutes of microwave cooking time.)

Place foil log directly on hot coals. Place drip pan on empty side of grill. Add 1 inch of water to drip pan. Place turkey directly on cooking grid over drip pan. Cover.

Grill for 1 hour 10 minutes to 1 hour 40 minutes, or until internal temperature in meaty portions of thighs registers 185°F, rotating turkey once. Let turkey stand, tented with foil, for 10 minutes before carving.

Per Serving:			
Calories:	193	Cholesterol:	86 mg.
Protein:	33 g.	Sodium:	79 mg.
Carbohydrate:	—	Exchanges:	4 lean meat
Fat:	6 g.		

Glazed Turkey & Peaches

1 can (16 oz.) peach halves in extra-light syrup, drained (reserve juice)	2 tablespoons margarine or butter
⅓ cup packed brown sugar	¼ teaspoon ground cinnamon
	2 turkey tenderloins (12 oz. each)

4 servings

Prepare grill for medium direct heat. Place reserved peach syrup in 2-cup measure. Set peach halves aside. Add sugar, margarine and cinnamon to peach syrup. Mix well. Microwave at High for 3 to 4 minutes, or until margarine is melted, stirring once. Set aside.

Arrange tenderloins in 8-inch square baking dish. Cover with wax paper. Microwave at 70% (Medium High) for 5 to 6 minutes, or until edges are no longer pink, turning over once.

Place tenderloins and peach halves on cooking grid. Grill, covered, for 10 to 14 minutes, or until meat is no longer pink, juices run clear, and internal temperature registers 175°F. Turn tenderloins and peach halves frequently and baste with peach syrup mixture several times.

Per Serving:			
Calories:	342	Cholesterol:	106 mg.
Protein:	39 g.	Sodium:	143 mg.
Carbohydrate:	31 g.	Exchanges:	4½ lean meat, 2 fruit
Fat:	7 g.		

Chicken Fajitas

2 boneless whole chicken
  breasts (8 to 10 oz. each),
  split in half, skin removed
1 cup Tequila Marinade
  (page 78), divided
1 medium green pepper, sliced
  into thin rings
1 medium onion, thinly sliced,
  separated into rings
4 flour tortillas, 8-inch

4 servings

Per Serving:	
Calories:	374
Protein:	41 g.
Carbohydrate:	23 g.
Fat:	11 g.
Cholesterol:	107 mg.
Sodium:	163 mg.
Exchanges:	1 starch, 4½ lean meat, 1½ vegetable

In large food-storage bag, combine chicken and ¾ cup marinade. Chill remaining marinade. Secure bag. Chill at least 2 hours, turning bag over once or twice. Prepare grill for low direct heat.

In 8-inch square baking dish, arrange chicken breasts with meaty portions toward outside edges. Pour marinade over chicken. Cover with wax paper. Microwave at High for 4 to 6 minutes, or until exterior of meat is no longer pink, rearranging chicken breasts once.

Place on cooking grid. Grill, uncovered, for 8 to 12 minutes, or until chicken is no longer pink and juices run clear, turning once. Wrap grilled chicken in foil to keep warm. Set aside.

In 1-quart casserole, combine remaining ¼ cup marinade, pepper and onion. Cover. Microwave at High for 5 to 7 minutes, or until pepper and onion are tender-crisp, stirring once or twice. Set aside.

Place tortillas between 2 dampened paper towels. Microwave at High for 45 seconds to 1 minute, or until tortillas are warm to the touch.

Cut each chicken breast half into thin strips. Place strips in warm tortilla. Top with one-fourth of pepper and onion mixture. Fold up from bottom. Fold in sides and secure with wooden pick, leaving top open. Top with salsa, sour cream and guacamole, if desired.

Steak Fajitas: Prepare grill for high direct heat. Follow recipe above, except substitute 1½ lbs. beef flank steak for chicken. Marinate 6 hours or overnight. Do not microwave steak before grilling. Place steak on cooking grid. Grill, covered, for 10 to 14 minutes, or until desired doneness. Let stand, tented with foil, for 10 minutes. Continue with recipe above.

Turkey Burgers ▲

1	lb. ground turkey
½	cup crushed herb-seasoned stuffing mix
⅓	cup chopped red onion
1	egg
¼	teaspoon garlic powder
¼	teaspoon salt

4 servings

Prepare grill for medium direct heat. In medium mixing bowl, combine all ingredients. Mix well. Shape mixture into four 4-inch round patties. Arrange patties on microwave roasting rack. Cover with wax paper. Microwave at 70% (Medium High) for 4 to 5 minutes, or until edges of patties are no longer pink, rotating rack once. Place patties on cooking grid. Grill, covered, for 5 minutes, or until patties are firm and juices run clear, turning patties over once. Serve on buns with mayonnaise, horse-radish sauce or catsup.

Per Serving:

Calories:	235	Cholesterol:	134 mg.
Protein:	29 g.	Sodium:	444 mg.
Carbohydrate:	14 g.	Exchanges:	1 starch, 3 lean meat
Fat:	6 g.		

Oriental Chicken Wings

2	lbs. chicken wings
2	cups Oriental Marinade (page 79), divided

6 servings

Per Serving:

Calories:	163
Protein:	15 g.
Carbohydrate:	14 g.
Fat:	5 g.
Cholesterol:	42 mg.
Sodium:	101 mg.
Exchanges:	2 lean meat, 1 fruit

Prepare grill for medium direct heat. Cut each chicken wing into 3 pieces, separating at joints. Discard wing tips.

In large plastic food-storage bag, combine chicken and 1 cup marinade. Refrigerate remaining marinade. Secure bag. Chill at least 2 hours or overnight, turning bag over once or twice.

Pour chicken wings and marinade into 3-quart casserole. Cover with wax paper. Microwave at High for 12 to 16 minutes, or until exterior of meat is no longer pink, stirring twice. Place wings on cooking grid. Grill, uncovered, for about 10 minutes, or until meat is no longer pink and juices run clear, basting with remaining 1 cup marinade and turning frequently.

Teriyaki Pork Kabobs

8 wooden skewers, 12-inch

Marinade:
⅓ cup soy sauce
¼ cup packed brown sugar
¼ cup lemon juice
¼ cup vegetable oil
1 teaspoon finely chopped
    gingerroot

1-lb. pork tenderloin, cut into
    24 pieces (about 1-inch)
2 large carrots, cut into 8
    lengths (2-inch lengths)
¼ cup water, divided
1 medium green pepper, cut
    into 12 chunks

4 servings

Soak skewers in water for ½ hour before grilling kabobs. In medium mixing bowl, combine marinade ingredients. Mix well. Microwave at High for 1 to 1½ minutes, or until sugar is dissolved, stirring once. Add pork. Stir to coat. Cover with plastic wrap. Chill at least 2 hours or overnight.

Prepare grill for low direct heat. In 1-quart casserole, place carrots and 2 tablespoons water. Cover. Microwave at High for 5 to 8 minutes, or until tender, stirring once. Rinse with cold water. Drain and set aside. In same 1-quart casserole, combine pepper chunks and remaining 2 tablespoons water. Cover. Microwave at High for 3 to 4 minutes, or until tender, stirring once. Rinse with cold water. Drain.

Place 2 wooden skewers side by side. Thread 1 pork cube, 1 pepper chunk, 1 pork cube, 1 carrot length, 1 pork cube, 1 pepper chunk, 1 pork cube, 1 carrot length, 1 pork cube, 1 pepper chunk and 1 pork cube. Repeat with remaining ingredients. Place kabobs on cooking grid. Grill, covered, for 12 to 15 minutes, or until pork is no longer pink, turning 2 or 3 times.

Per Serving:

Calories:	218	Cholesterol:	79 mg.	
Protein:	26 g.	Sodium:	422 mg.	
Carbohydrate:	11 g.	Exchanges:	3 lean meat, 2 vegetable	
Fat:	8 g.			

Beer-basted Brats ▶

6 fresh bratwurst (about 1½ lbs.)
½ cup beer
1 small onion, sliced and
    separated into rings

6 servings

Prepare grill for medium direct heat. In 8-inch square baking dish, arrange brats in single layer. Pour beer over brats. Sprinkle with onion. Cover with plastic wrap. Microwave at High for 8 to 11 minutes, or until brats are firm and no longer pink, rearranging once.

Place brats on cooking grid. Grill, uncovered, for 5 to 8 minutes, or until brats are golden brown, turning frequently.

Per Serving:
Calories:	352
Protein:	16 g.
Carbohydrate:	4 g.
Fat:	29 g.
Cholesterol:	68 mg.
Sodium:	634 mg.
Exchanges:	2 high-fat meat, ½ vegetable, 3 fat

Quick Cajun Chops

Seasoning:

1 teaspoon dried oregano
    leaves
½ teaspoon chili powder
¼ teaspoon garlic salt
¼ teaspoon ground cumin
⅛ teaspoon cayenne (optional)

4 pork chops (4 oz. each), ½
    inch thick

4 servings

Prepare grill for low direct heat. In small bowl, combine seasoning ingredients. Mix well. Rub evenly on both sides of each chop.

Arrange chops on microwave roasting rack with meaty portions toward outside. Cover with wax paper. Microwave at 70% (Medium High) for 8 to 10 minutes, or until edges of chops are no longer pink, turning chops over once.

Place on cooking grid. Grill, covered, for 7 to 12 minutes, or until meat near bone is no longer pink and chops are golden brown, turning chops over once. Serve with salsa sauce, if desired.

Per Serving:
Calories:	222	Cholesterol:	80 mg.
Protein:	25 g.	Sodium:	174 mg.
Carbohydrate:	1 g.	Exchanges:	3 medium-fat meat
Fat:	13 g.		

Micro-grilled Fruits & Vegetables

Honey-glazed Pears ▶

4   medium fresh pears (about 8
    oz. each), cored and cut in
    half lengthwise
¼   cup water
2   tablespoons frozen orange
    juice concentrate
2   tablespoons honey
1   tablespoon packed brown
    sugar
1   tablespoon snipped fresh
    mint leaves

4 servings

Prepare grill for medium direct
heat. In 10-inch square casserole, arrange pear halves cut-
sides-up. Pour water over pears.
Cover. Microwave at High for 5 to
7 minutes, or until fruit is tender-
crisp, rearranging pieces once.
Drain. Set aside.

In 1-cup measure, combine concentrate, honey and sugar. Mix
well. Microwave at High for 1 to
1½ minutes, or until sugar is dissolved. Stir in mint.

Brush pear halves with juice
mixture. Place pear halves cut-
sides-down on cooking grid.
Grill, covered, for about 4 minutes, or until fruit is hot, turning
and basting with juice mixture
frequently.

Per Serving:	
Calories:	141
Protein:	1 g.
Carbohydrate:	36 g.
Fat:	1 g.
Cholesterol:	—
Sodium:	2 mg.
Exchanges:	2½ fruit

◄ Orange-glazed Pineapple

1 fresh pineapple (2½ to 3 lbs.)
½ cup orange marmalade
¼ cup pineapple or orange
    juice
½ teaspoon grated lime peel

8 servings

Prepare grill for medium direct heat. Cut off crown and stem end of pineapple. Stand pineapple upright and slice off rind in narrow, lengthwise strips, leaving as much fruit as possible.

Remove the eyes by making diagonal cuts on both sides of each row of eyes. Slice pineapple into ½-inch rings. Remove core from rings by cutting around it with small knife. Set rings aside.

In 2-cup measure, combine the marmalade, juice and peel. Mix well. Microwave at High for 1 to 2 minutes, or until marmalade is melted and mixture can be stirred smooth.

Brush pineapple slices with marmalade mixture. Place pineapple slices on cooking grid. Grill, covered, for 4 to 7 minutes, or until pineapple is hot, turning and basting with marmalade mixture frequently.

Per Serving:	
Calories:	97
Protein:	1 g.
Carbohydrate:	26 g.
Fat:	1 g.
Cholesterol:	—
Sodium:	4 mg.
Exchanges:	1½ fruit

Skewered New Potatoes, Peppers & Onions ▲

8   wooden skewers, 12-inch
12   small new potatoes, 1½-inch
    diameter (about 1½ lbs.)
12   fresh pearl onions
¼   cup vegetable oil
2   tablespoons red wine vinegar
2   tablespoons soy sauce
1   clove garlic, minced
1   medium green pepper, cut
    into 12 chunks

4 servings

Soak skewers in water for ½ hour before grilling kabobs. Prepare grill for medium direct heat. In 2-quart casserole, place potatoes and onions. Set aside.

In 1-cup measure, combine oil, vinegar, soy sauce and garlic. Mix well. Add to potatoes and onions. Toss to coat. Cover. Microwave at High for 13 to 15 minutes, or until potatoes are tender, stirring twice. Add pepper chunks. Re-cover. Let stand for 5 minutes. Drain.

Place 2 skewers side by side. For each kabob, thread 1 potato, 1 pepper chunk and 1 onion. Repeat sequence twice. Repeat with remaining ingredients. Grill kabobs, covered, for 6 to 9 minutes, or until hot and golden brown, turning twice.

Per Serving:			
Calories:	278	Cholesterol:	—
Protein:	5 g.	Sodium:	526 mg.
Carbohydrate:	35 g.	Exchanges:	2 starch, 1 vegetable, 2 fat
Fat:	14 g.		

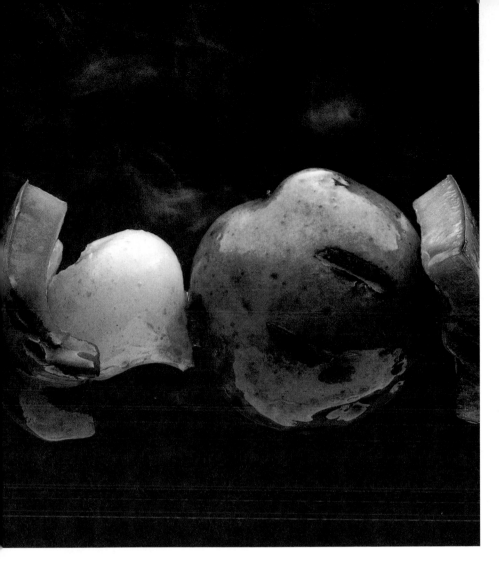

Grilled Cheddar Cauliflower

1 medium head cauliflower (about 1 lb.)
¼ cup margarine or butter
½ teaspoon grated lemon peel
½ teaspoon dried thyme leaves
½ cup finely shredded Cheddar cheese

4 servings

Prepare grill for medium direct heat. Break off outer leaves and trim stem close to base of cauliflower head. Wash in cool water. Shake off excess water. Wrap head in plastic wrap.

Place cauliflower on paper plate stem-side-up. Microwave at High for 3 minutes. Turn cauliflower over. Microwave at High for 4 minutes. Let stand, wrapped, for 5 minutes.

In 1-cup measure, microwave margarine at High for 1¼ to 1½ minutes, or until melted. Add lemon peel and thyme. Mix well. Brush cauliflower with margarine mixture.

Place cauliflower stem-side-down on cooking grid. Grill, covered, for about 5 minutes, or until cauliflower is fork-tender near base, basting frequently with margarine mixture.

Place grilled cauliflower on serving platter. Sprinkle with cheese. Cover loosely with foil. Let stand for 5 minutes, or until cheese is melted.

Per Serving:	
Calories:	180
Protein:	5 g.
Carbohydrate:	5 g.
Fat:	16 g.
Cholesterol:	15 mg.
Sodium:	236 mg.
Exchanges:	½ high-fat meat, 1 vegetable, 2½ fat

Rosemary Stuffed Grilled Potatoes

4 baking potatoes (8 to 10 oz. each)
1 cup thin green pepper strips
1 small onion, thinly sliced
1 teaspoon dried rosemary leaves, crushed
½ teaspoon garlic salt
4 teaspoons olive oil

4 servings

Prepare grill for medium direct heat. Pierce potatoes with fork. Arrange in circle on paper towel in microwave oven. Microwave at High for 9 to 12 minutes, or until potatoes are very hot and yield to slight pressure. Cool slightly.

Make 3 diagonal cuts at 1-inch intervals to within ½ inch of bottom of each potato. Place pepper strips and onion slices evenly between slits in each potato. Place each potato on sheet of heavy-duty foil. Sprinkle evenly with rosemary, garlic salt and oil.

Wrap foil around potato. Place potatoes on cooking grid. Grill, covered, for 20 to 25 minutes, or until tender.

Per Serving:			
Calories:	233	Cholesterol:	—
Protein:	5 g.	Sodium:	246 mg.
Carbohydrate:	44 g.	Exchanges:	2½ starch, 1 vegetable, 1 fat
Fat:	5 g.		

Chive-seasoned Potato Slices ▶

2 baking potatoes (about 8 oz. each), cut lengthwise into ¼-inch slices
½ cup water
¼ cup margarine or butter

1 tablespoon snipped fresh chives or 1 teaspoon freeze-dried chives
1 clove garlic, minced

4 servings

Prepare grill for medium direct heat. In 2-quart casserole, combine potatoes and water. Cover. Microwave at High for 8 to 10 minutes, or until tender, stirring once. Let stand, covered, for 5 minutes. Drain.

In 2-cup measure, place margarine. Microwave at High for 1¼ to 1½ minutes, or until melted. Add chives and garlic. Mix well. Brush potato slices with chive butter.

Place potato slices on cooking grid. Grill, covered, for 13 to 15 minutes, or until potatoes are lightly browned, turning and basting with chive butter frequently. Sprinkle with salt, if desired.

Per Serving:			
Calories:	193	Cholesterol:	—
Protein:	3 g.	Sodium:	141 mg.
Carbohydrate:	21 g.	Exchanges:	1½ starch, 2 fat
Fat:	12 g.		

Grilled Yellow Squash & Zucchini Fans

2 medium yellow summer squash (about 8 oz. each)
2 medium zucchini (about 8 oz. each)
½ cup Italian dressing

4 servings

Per Serving:	
Calories:	73
Protein:	2 g.
Carbohydrate:	9 g.
Fat:	4 g.
Cholesterol:	—
Sodium:	65 mg.
Exchanges:	1½ vegetable, ½ fat

How to Make Grilled Yellow Squash & Zucchini Fans ▲

Prepare grill for medium direct heat. Cut each squash lengthwise into ¼-inch strips, starting 1 inch from stem end (squash must stay intact).

Place squash in 10-inch square casserole. Pour dressing over squash. Cover. Microwave at High for 8 to 10 minutes, or until squash is pliable, rearranging once. Remove squash from casserole. Reserve dressing.

Arrange squash on cooking grid so slices fan out. Grill, covered, for 7 to 9 minutes, or until squash is tender, turning over and basting with dressing twice. Serve sprinkled with grated Parmesan cheese, if desired.

Roasted Broccoli ▶

1 to 1½ lbs. fresh broccoli, cut   ½ cup Italian dressing
   into spears

4 servings

Prepare grill for medium direct heat. In 10-inch square casserole, arrange broccoli in single layer. Pour dressing over broccoli. Cover. Microwave at High for 6 to 9 minutes, or until broccoli is tender-crisp, rearranging spears once.

Place broccoli spears on cooking grid. Grill, covered, for 4 to 5 minutes, or until spears are tender, turning and basting with dressing frequently.

Per Serving:			
Calories:	69	Cholesterol:	—
Protein:	3 g.	Sodium:	90 mg.
Carbohydrate:	8 g.	Exchanges:	1½ vegetable, ½ fat
Fat:	4 g.		

Grilled Italian-seasoned Eggplant ▶

1 eggplant (1 lb.)   ½ cup Italian dressing

4 servings

Prepare grill for medium direct heat. Slice stem from eggplant. Cut eggplant lengthwise into ½-inch slices.

Place slices in 10-inch square casserole. Pour dressing over eggplant. Cover. Microwave at High for 12 to 18 minutes, or until eggplant is almost tender and translucent, rearranging twice.

Place eggplant slices on cooking grid. Grill, covered, for 7 to 8 minutes, or until tender, turning slices over and basting with dressing twice. Serve sprinkled with grated Parmesan cheese, if desired.

Per Serving:			
Calories:	65	Cholesterol:	—
Protein:	1 g.	Sodium:	64 mg.
Carbohydrate:	8 g.	Exchanges:	1½ vegetable, ½ fat
Fat:	4 g.		

Quick Summer Entrées

Dilled Salmon
with Tricolored
Peppers

Ratatouille Tart

1 frozen unbaked ready-to-use
   puff pastry sheet (about
   ½ lb.)
1 egg
1 tablespoon water
1 pkg. (3 oz.) cream cheese
½ cup ricotta cheese
2 teaspoons chopped fresh
   rosemary leaves
2 teaspoons fresh thyme leaves
½ teaspoon salt, divided
1 medium eggplant (1 lb.), cut
   in half lengthwise and sliced
   (½-inch slices)
2 tablespoons olive oil
8 sprigs fresh rosemary
8 sprigs fresh thyme
1 clove garlic, minced
½ cup thinly sliced zucchini
½ cup thinly sliced yellow
   summer squash
2 Roma tomatoes, thinly sliced

6 servings

Per Serving:	
Calories:	335
Protein:	8 g.
Carbohydrate:	24 g.
Fat:	23 g.
Cholesterol:	68 mg.
Sodium:	452 mg.
Exchanges:	1 starch, 2 vegetable, 4½ fat

How to Make Ratatouille Tart

Heat conventional oven to 350°F. Defrost pastry at room temperature for about 20 minutes. Unfold pastry. Place on lightly floured board. Roll into 14 × 11-inch rectangle. Cut 1-inch strips from each side of rectangle. Set strips aside.

Place rectangle on large baking sheet. Prick generously with fork. In 1-cup measure, combine egg and water. Beat with fork until blended. Brush rectangle lightly with egg mixture. Place strips on rectangle so outside edges meet. Trim to fit.

Brush tops of strips evenly with egg mixture. Bake for 5 minutes. If bottom puffs, prick with fork until pastry deflates. Bake for 15 to 17 minutes longer, or until pastry is light golden brown. Cool completely.

Place cream cheese in small mixing bowl. Microwave at High for 15 to 30 seconds, or until softened. Add ricotta cheese, rosemary and thyme leaves, and ¼ teaspoon salt. Mix well. Spread cream cheese mixture evenly in cooled tart shell.

Combine eggplant, oil, rosemary and thyme sprigs, garlic and remaining ¼ teaspoon salt in 2-quart casserole. Cover. Microwave at High for 11 to 15 minutes, or until eggplant is translucent, stirring 3 times.

Add zucchini and yellow squash. Re-cover. Microwave at High for 1 minute. Let stand for 5 minutes. Arrange eggplant, zucchini, yellow squash and tomato slices diagonally in tart shell. Serve immediately or cover with plastic wrap and chill up to 4 hours.

99

Dilled Salmon with Tricolored Peppers

- 4 to 6 fresh dill sprigs
- 12 oz. salmon fillet, skin removed, cut into serving-size pieces
- ½ cup thin strips red onion (1½ × ¼-inch)
- 1½ cups thin strips red, yellow and green pepper (1½ × ¼-inch)
- ½ cup seeded chopped tomato
- 2 tablespoons lemon juice
- 2 tablespoons lime juice
- ¼ cup sliced green onions
- 1 tablespoon olive or vegetable oil
- 1 tablespoon snipped fresh dill weed
- 1 small fresh chili pepper, seeded and chopped
- ¼ teaspoon salt
- 3 to 6 drops red pepper sauce

4 servings

In 8-inch square baking dish, arrange dill sprigs in even layer. Place salmon pieces over dill sprigs. Cover with plastic wrap. Microwave at 70% (Medium High) for 5 to 8 minutes, or until fish flakes easily with fork, rotating and rearranging pieces once or twice. Chill about 2 hours, or until cold.

In medium mixing bowl, combine remaining ingredients. Mix well. Chill at least 2 hours to blend flavors. Arrange pepper mixture evenly on each of 4 serving plates. Top pepper mixture with salmon fillets.

Per Serving:	
Calories:	208
Protein:	19 g.
Carbohydrate:	8 g.
Fat:	11 g.
Cholesterol:	53 mg.
Sodium:	246 mg.
Exchanges:	2 lean meat, 1½ vegetable, 1 fat

Orange Roughy with Berry-Nut Salsa ▲

 1 cup sliced fresh strawberries
 ½ cup fresh blueberries
 ½ cup fresh raspberries
 ¼ cup chopped pecans
 2 tablespoons sliced green
    onion
 2 tablespoons raspberry or
    white vinegar
 2 teaspoons packed brown
    sugar
 1 tablespoon vegetable oil
 12 oz. orange roughy fillets,
    about ½ inch thick, cut into
    serving-size pieces

                    4 servings

In small mixing bowl, combine berries, pecans and onion. Toss gently to combine. In 1-cup measure, combine vinegar and sugar. Add oil. Blend with whisk. Add vinegar mixture to berry mixture. Toss gently to coat. Set aside.

In 8-inch square baking dish, arrange fillets in even layer. Cover with wax paper. Microwave at High for 3 to 4½ minutes, or until fish flakes easily with fork. Let stand, covered, for 3 minutes.

Place fillets on serving plates. Top each serving with one-fourth of salsa.

Per Serving:			
Calories:	233	Cholesterol:	17 mg.
Protein:	14 g.	Sodium:	56 mg.
Carbohydrate:	13 g.	Exchanges:	2 lean meat, 1 fruit, 1½ fat
Fat:	15 g.		

Jalapeño, Peach, Shrimp & Rice

 12 oz. large shrimp, shelled and
    deveined
 2 cups cooked brown rice
 2 medium peaches, peeled
    and cut into chunks (¾-inch
    chunks)
 ¼ cup chopped red pepper
 ¼ cup sliced green onions
 1 small jalapeño pepper, finely
    chopped

Dressing:

 ¼ cup vegetable oil
 2 tablespoons red wine vinegar
 1 teaspoon ground cumin
 1 clove garlic, minced
 ½ teaspoon grated orange peel
 ½ teaspoon salt

                    4 servings

In 9-inch round cake dish, arrange shrimp in single layer. Cover with plastic wrap. Microwave at 70% (Medium High) for 3 to 5 minutes, or until shrimp are opaque, stirring once to rearrange. Let stand, covered, for 1 to 2 minutes. Drain. Rinse with cold water.

In medium mixing bowl, combine shrimp, rice, peaches, red pepper, onions and jalapeño pepper. Mix well. Set aside.

In 1-cup measure, combine dressing ingredients. Add to rice mixture. Toss to coat. Cover with plastic wrap. Chill about 4 hours, or until cold.

Per Serving:			
Calories:	337	Cholesterol:	97 mg.
Protein:	16 g.	Sodium:	359 mg.
Carbohydrate:	34 g.	Exchanges:	1½ starch, 1½ lean meat,
Fat:	16 g.		1 vegetable, ½ fruit, 2 fat

Garden Marinara Sauce

4 to 5 medium tomatoes (about 2 lbs.)
4 cups hot water
4 cups ice water
⅓ cup chopped red onion
2 tablespoons olive oil
1 clove garlic, minced
1 can (8 oz.) tomato sauce
¼ cup tomato paste
3 tablespoons snipped fresh basil leaves
½ teaspoon sugar
½ teaspoon salt
¼ teaspoon crushed red pepper flakes
1 medium zucchini, cut in half lengthwise and thinly sliced (about 1 cup)
1 medium yellow summer squash, cut in half lengthwise and thinly sliced (about 1 cup)
2 tablespoons water
12 oz. hot cooked pasta
Freshly grated Parmesan cheese (optional)

6 servings

Using sharp knife, cut crossmark on bottom of each tomato. Set aside. Place hot water in 2-quart casserole or 8-cup measure. Cover with plastic wrap. Microwave at High for 6 to 11 minutes, or until water boils. Add tomatoes. Let stand for 1½ minutes.

Place ice water in medium mixing bowl. Immerse tomatoes briefly in ice water. Core and peel. Cut in half crosswise. Remove and discard seeds. Cut tomatoes into ½-inch chunks. Set aside.

In 2-quart casserole, place onion, oil and garlic. Cover. Microwave at High for 3 to 4 minutes, or until onion is tender, stirring once. Add tomatoes, the tomato sauce, paste, basil, sugar, salt and red pepper flakes. Mix well. Microwave at High for 10 to 12 minutes, or until mixture is desired consistency, stirring 2 or 3 times. Cover. Set aside.

In 1-quart casserole, place zucchini, yellow squash and 2 tablespoons water. Cover. Microwave at High for 4 to 5 minutes, or until tender-crisp, stirring once. Drain. Add to tomato mixture. Mix well. Serve over hot cooked pasta. Sprinkle with Parmesan cheese.

Per Serving:			
Calories:	313	Cholesterol:	—
Protein:	10 g.	Sodium:	508 mg.
Carbohydrate:	57 g.	Exchanges:	2 starch, 5 vegetable, 1 fat
Fat:	6 g.		

Cold Tuna-stuffed Manicotti

8 uncooked manicotti shells

Filling:

6 oz. fresh asparagus spears, cut into ¾-inch lengths (about 1 cup)
2 tablespoons snipped fresh basil leaves
1 tablespoon olive oil
1 large clove garlic, minced
2 cans (6½ oz. each) solid white tuna, water pack, drained and flaked
⅓ cup mayonnaise
¼ cup chopped red onion

Topping:

1 cup quartered cherry tomatoes
2 tablespoons chopped red onion
2 tablespoons snipped fresh basil leaves
2 tablespoons olive oil
1 tablespoon red wine vinegar
⅛ teaspoon salt
⅛ teaspoon pepper

6 to 8 servings

Prepare manicotti shells as directed on package. Rinse with cold water. Drain. Cover with plastic wrap. Set aside.

In 1-quart casserole, combine asparagus, 2 tablespoons basil, 1 tablespoon oil and the garlic. Cover. Microwave at High for 4 to 6 minutes, or until asparagus is tender-crisp, stirring once.

Place tuna in medium mixing bowl. Add asparagus mixture to tuna. Add mayonnaise and onion. Mix well. Spoon filling evenly into cooked shells. Arrange stuffed shells on serving platter.

In small mixing bowl, combine topping ingredients. Toss to coat. Spoon topping over stuffed shells. Cover with plastic wrap. Chill about 2 hours, or until cold.

Cold Salmon-stuffed Manicotti: Follow recipe above, except substitute 2 cans (6½ oz. each) skinless, boneless salmon, drained, for tuna.

Per Serving:			
Calories:	243	Cholesterol:	35 mg.
Protein:	16 g.	Sodium:	106 mg.
Carbohydrate:	15 g.	Exchanges:	1 starch, 2 lean meat, 1½ fat
Fat:	13 g.		

Icebox Club Salad

- 4 slices bacon
- 8 cups torn Bibb lettuce, divided
- 1 pkg. (10 oz.) frozen tiny peas
- ½ lb. fully cooked ham, cut into ½-inch cubes
- ½ lb. fully cooked turkey, cut into ½-inch cubes
- 1 cup shredded Swiss cheese (4 oz.)
- 1 cup seeded chopped tomato
- ½ cup thinly sliced red onion

Dressing:

- 1 cup mayonnaise or salad dressing
- ½ cup plain low-fat yogurt or sour cream
- 1 tablespoon prepared mustard
- 1 teaspoon dried basil leaves

8 servings

Layer 3 paper towels on plate. Arrange bacon on paper towels. Cover with another paper towel. Microwave at High for 3 to 6 minutes, or until bacon is brown and crisp. Cool slightly. Crumble. Set aside.

In 12 × 8-inch glass baking dish, spread 4 cups lettuce in even layer. Top evenly with peas, ham, turkey, cheese, tomato and onion. Top evenly with remaining lettuce. Set aside.

In medium mixing bowl, combine dressing ingredients. Mix well. Spread dressing evenly over top of salad. Sprinkle with crumbled bacon. Cover with plastic wrap. Chill at least 4 hours, or until cold. Serve in squares.

Per Serving:	
Calories:	415
Protein:	23 g.
Carbohydrate:	11 g.
Fat:	31 g.
Cholesterol:	70 mg.
Sodium:	686 mg.
Exchanges:	3 medium-fat meat, ½ starch, 1 vegetable, 3 fat

Spanish-style Chicken Breasts ▲

- 2 boneless whole chicken breasts (8 to 10 oz. each), split in half, skin removed
- 1 medium green pepper, cut into chunks (¾-inch chunks)
- ½ cup sliced red onion
- ¼ cup pimiento-stuffed green olives, cut in half
- ¼ cup fresh oregano leaves, loosely packed
- 2 cloves garlic, minced
- ⅓ cup oil and vinegar dressing
- 4 Roma tomatoes, quartered

4 servings

In 11 × 7-inch baking dish, arrange chicken breasts with meaty portions toward outside edges. Top evenly with pepper, onion, olives, oregano, garlic and dressing. Cover with plastic wrap.

Microwave at High for 9 to 12 minutes, or until meat is no longer pink and juices run clear, rearranging breasts twice. Sprinkle with tomatoes. Recover. Chill about 6 hours, or until cold.

Per Serving:			
Calories:	274	Cholesterol:	72 mg.
Protein:	28 g.	Sodium:	426 mg.
Carbohydrate:	9 g.	Exchanges:	3 lean meat, 2 vegetable, 1 fat
Fat:	14 g.		

Curried Beef, Broccoli & Cauliflower Salad

Dressing:

½ cup olive oil
2 tablespoons white wine vinegar
1 tablespoon lemon juice
2 teaspoons curry powder
1 clove garlic, minced
½ teaspoon salt
¼ teaspoon crushed red pepper flakes
⅛ teaspoon pepper

Salad:

½-lb. boneless beef sirloin steak
2 cups fresh cauliflowerets
2 cups fresh broccoli flowerets
1 cup julienne carrot (2 × ¼-inch strips)
2 tablespoons water
1 cup sliced celery (¼-inch slices)
½ cup thinly sliced red onion

4 servings

In 2-cup measure, combine dressing ingredients. Mix well. Microwave at High for 1½ to 2 minutes, or just until dressing is warm, stirring once. Place sirloin in large plastic food-storage bag. Add 2 tablespoons dressing mixture to bag. Secure bag. Turn bag to coat sirloin. Set bag and remaining dressing aside.

In 2-quart casserole, combine cauliflower, broccoli, carrot and water. Cover. Microwave at High for 4 to 5 minutes, or until vegetables are very hot and colors brighten, stirring twice. Rinse with cold water. Drain.

In large mixing bowl or salad bowl, combine vegetable mixture, celery, onion and remaining dressing. Toss to combine. Set aside.

Remove sirloin from bag. Place on microwave roasting rack. Microwave at 70% (Medium High) for 4 to 5 minutes, or until medium doneness, rotating once. Cool slightly. Slice into thin strips. Add to salad. Toss to combine. Cover with plastic wrap. Chill at least 4 hours or overnight.

Per Serving:			
Calories:	382	Cholesterol:	32 mg.
Protein:	15 g.	Sodium:	353 mg.
Carbohydrate:	12 g.	Exchanges:	1½ medium-fat meat, 2½ vegetable,
Fat:	32 g.		4½ fat

Simple
Side Dishes

Herbed Artichokes

Hot Sweet Carrots & Broccoli

3 cups fresh broccoli flowerets
1 pkg. (12 oz.) fresh baby carrots
¼ cup water
2 tablespoons margarine or butter
2 tablespoons packed brown sugar
1 teaspoon dry mustard
¼ teaspoon red pepper sauce
¼ teaspoon salt

6 to 8 servings

In 2-quart casserole, combine broccoli, carrots and water. Cover. Microwave at High for 6 to 9 minutes, or until carrots are tender-crisp, stirring twice. Let stand, covered, for 3 minutes. Drain. Set aside.

In 1-cup measure, microwave margarine at High for 45 seconds to 1 minute, or until melted. Stir in remaining ingredients. Pour over broccoli mixture. Toss to coat.

Per Serving:			
Calories:	66	Cholesterol:	—
Protein:	1 g.	Sodium:	122 mg.
Carbohydrate:	9 g.	Exchanges:	2 vegetable, ½ fat
Fat:	3 g.		

Asparagus with Summer Hollandaise

1 lb. fresh asparagus spears
¼ cup water
2 egg yolks, slightly beaten
1 tablespoon fresh lemon juice
⅛ teaspoon salt
  Dash cayenne
5 tablespoons margarine or
  butter
⅓ cup peeled seeded finely
  chopped cucumber
2 teaspoons snipped fresh dill
  weed

4 servings

In 11 × 7-inch baking dish, place asparagus with buds toward center. Add water. Cover with plastic wrap. Microwave at High for 6½ to 9½ minutes, or until tender-crisp, rearranging spears once. Drain. Place asparagus on serving platter. Cover with plastic wrap to keep warm. Set aside.

Combine egg yolks, lemon juice, salt and cayenne in food processor or blender. Blend about 5 seconds, or until smooth. In 2-cup measure, microwave margarine at High for 1½ to 1¾ minutes, or until melted. Blend egg yolk mixture at low speed of food processor or blender. Add melted margarine to mixture in a slow, steady stream. Continue blending until sauce thickens. Stir in cucumber and dill weed. Pour over asparagus. Serve immediately.

Per Serving:			
Calories:	186	Cholesterol:	136 mg.
Protein:	5 g.	Sodium:	237 mg.
Carbohydrate:	5 g.	Exchanges:	1 vegetable, 3½ fat
Fat:	17 g.		

Cold Caraway Cauliflower ▲

4	cups fresh cauliflowerets	½	teaspoon whole caraway
¼	cup water		seed
1	cup sliced radishes	¼	teaspoon salt
⅓	cup ranch dressing		

6 to 8 servings

In 2-quart casserole, combine cauliflower and water. Cover. Microwave at High for 8 to 10 minutes, or until tender-crisp. Let stand, covered, for 3 minutes. Rinse with cold water. Drain. Add radishes to cauliflower.

In small bowl, combine dressing, caraway seed and salt. Mix well. Add dressing to vegetables. Toss to coat. Chill at least 4 hours, or until vegetables are cold and flavors are blended.

Per Serving:			
Calories:	69	Cholesterol:	1 mg.
Protein:	2 g.	Sodium:	204 mg.
Carbohydrate:	5 g.	Exchanges:	1 vegetable, 1 fat
Fat:	5 g.		

Dilled Snap Peas ▲
& Radishes

1	lb. fresh sugar snap peas
½	cup water
½	cup plain yogurt
2	tablespoons mayonnaise
1	tablespoon snipped fresh dill weed
1	teaspoon sugar
¼	teaspoon salt
1	cup sliced radishes

4 servings

Per Serving:	
Calories:	127
Protein:	5 g.
Carbohydrate:	13 g.
Fat:	6 g.
Cholesterol:	6 mg.
Sodium:	199 mg.
Exchanges:	1 starch, 1 fat

How to Microwave Dilled Snap Peas & Radishes

Cut off end of each pea pod, leaving string attached. Pull string down pod. Cut off remaining end. In 2-quart casserole, place peas and water. Cover. Microwave at High for 5 to 6 minutes, or until peas are tender-crisp, stirring once. Rinse in cold water. Drain. Set aside.

Combine yogurt, mayonnaise, dill weed, sugar and salt in small mixing bowl. Mix well. Add yogurt mixture and radish slices to peas. Toss to coat. Cover. Chill about 3 hours, or until vegetables are cold and flavors are blended.

Pineapple-glazed Beets

1 lb. fresh beets (about 4 or 5)
½ cup water
2 tablespoons packed brown sugar
1 tablespoon cornstarch
¼ teaspoon salt
½ cup pineapple juice

4 servings

Wash beets gently to avoid breaking skins. Trim, leaving root ends and 1 to 2 inches of tops. Place beets in 2-quart casserole. Add water. Cover. Microwave at High for 15 to 20 minutes, or until tender, turning beets over and rotating casserole every 5 minutes.

Let stand, covered, for 3 to 5 minutes, or until cool enough to handle. Drain. Slip off skins and tops. Trim root ends. Cut into ¼-inch slices. Return to casserole. Re-cover. Set aside.

In 2-cup measure, combine sugar, cornstarch and salt. Stir in juice. Microwave at High for 1½ to 2½ minutes, or until mixture is thickened and translucent, stirring once. Pour sauce over beets. Toss gently to coat.

Per Serving:	
Calories:	100
Protein:	2 g.
Carbohydrate:	24 g.
Fat:	—
Cholesterol:	—
Sodium:	210 mg.
Exchanges:	3 vegetable, ½ fruit

Cilantro-Lime Beans

8 oz. fresh wax beans
8 oz. fresh green beans
1 can (4 oz.) chopped green
   chilies, drained
2 tablespoons margarine or
   butter
1 tablespoon snipped fresh
   cilantro leaves
2 teaspoons fresh lime juice
½ teaspoon sugar
¼ teaspoon salt

4 servings

Remove stem and tip ends from beans. In 2-quart casse-role, combine beans and remaining ingredients. Mix well. Cover. Microwave at High for 12 to 17 minutes, or until beans are tender-crisp, stirring once. Let stand, covered, for 2 to 3 minutes.

Per Serving:			
Calories:	98	Cholesterol:	—
Protein:	3 g.	Sodium:	202 mg.
Carbohydrate:	11 g.	Exchanges:	2 vegetable, 1 fat
Fat:	6 g.		

Confetti Corn ▶

4	slices bacon
1	pkg. (16 oz.) frozen corn
½	cup chopped green pepper
½	cup chopped red pepper
½	cup water
¼	teaspoon salt
⅛	teaspoon cayenne

6 servings

Arrange bacon on roasting rack. Cover with paper towel. Microwave at High for 3 to 6 minutes, or until bacon is brown and crisp. Set aside.

In 2-quart casserole, combine corn, peppers and water. Mix well. Cover. Microwave at High for 9 to 12 minutes, or until corn is hot, stirring twice. Drain.

Crumble bacon. Add bacon, salt and cayenne to corn mixture. Mix well. Serve immediately.

Per Serving:	
Calories:	95
Protein:	4 g.
Carbohydrate:	17 g.
Fat:	3 g.
Cholesterol:	4 mg.
Sodium:	154 mg.
Exchanges:	1 starch, ½ vegetable, ½ fat

Cold Marinated Corn

4	fresh ears corn on the cob, husked (7 to 8 oz. each)
¼	cup water
½	cup vegetable oil
¼	cup orange juice
1	tablespoon Dijon mustard
1	tablespoon honey
1	tablespoon snipped fresh chives
1	tablespoon snipped fresh dill weed
1	tablespoon snipped fresh parsley
½	teaspoon salt
¼	teaspoon pepper

4 servings

Arrange corn in 8-inch square baking dish. Add water. Cover with plastic wrap. Microwave at High for 7½ to 16 minutes, or until corn is tender, rearranging ears twice. Let stand for 5 minutes.

In 2-cup measure, combine remaining ingredients. Place corn in large plastic food-storage bag. Add juice mixture. Secure bag. Place bag in refrigerator. Chill 4 hours, or until cold, turning bag twice.

Per Serving:			
Calories:	113	Cholesterol:	—
Protein:	3 g.	Sodium:	106 mg.
Carbohydrate:	16 g.	Exchanges:	1 starch, 1½ fat
Fat:	8 g.		

Spinach-stuffed Peppers ▶

  3 green, red or yellow peppers
 ¼ cup water
  1 pkg. (10 oz.) frozen chopped
      spinach
 ½ cup chopped onion
  1 tablespoon margarine or
      butter
 ½ teaspoon salt
 ½ teaspoon pepper
 ¼ teaspoon garlic powder
  1 cup seeded chopped tomato
 ⅓ cup unseasoned dry bread
      crumbs
 ¼ cup shredded mozzarella
      cheese

6 servings

Per Serving:	
Calories:	75
Protein:	4 g.
Carbohydrate:	9 g.
Fat:	3 g.
Cholesterol:	3 mg.
Sodium:	277 mg.
Exchanges:	2 vegetable, ½ fat

How to Microwave Spinach-stuffed Peppers

Cut each pepper in half lengthwise; remove seeds. In 10-inch square casserole, arrange peppers cut-sides-up. Sprinkle with water. Cover with plastic wrap. Microwave at High for 6 to 8 minutes, or until tender-crisp, rearranging once. Drain. Set aside.

Herbed Artichokes ▲

2 tablespoons margarine or
    butter
1 tablespoon fresh lemon juice
1 tablespoon snipped fresh
    chives

½ teaspoon dry mustard
2 fresh artichokes (8 to 10 oz.
    each)

4 servings

In 1-cup measure, microwave margarine at High for 45 seconds to 1 minute, or until melted. Stir in juice, chives and mustard. Set aside.

Trim each artichoke stem close to base. Cut 1 inch off tops, and trim ends off each leaf. Cut each artichoke lengthwise into fourths. Remove some of center leaves and scrape out choke from each piece.

Arrange artichokes in 8-inch square baking dish. Drizzle with margarine mixture. Cover with plastic wrap. Microwave at High for 8 to 10 minutes, or until artichokes are tender, rearranging pieces once.

Per Serving:			
Calories:	119	Cholesterol:	—
Protein:	4 g.	Sodium:	166 mg.
Carbohydrate:	16 g.	Exchanges:	3 vegetable, 1 fat
Fat:	6 g.		

Place spinach in 2-quart casserole. Cover. Microwave at High for 4 to 6 minutes, or until spinach is defrosted. Drain, pressing to remove excess moisture. Set aside.

Combine onion, margarine, salt, pepper and garlic powder in 2-quart casserole. Cover. Microwave at High for 3 to 4 minutes, or until onions are tender, stirring once. Add spinach, tomato and bread crumbs to onion mixture. Mix well.

Spoon spinach mixture evenly into peppers. Re-cover. Microwave at High for 4 to 6 minutes, or until peppers are tender and spinach mixture is hot. Sprinkle cheese evenly over peppers. Microwave at High for 1½ to 2 minutes, or until cheese is melted.

Colorful Marinated Vegetables ▲

1 lb. fresh Brussels sprouts,
   cut in half
1 cup sliced carrots (¼ inch
   thick)
½ cup thinly sliced onion,
   separated into rings
½ cup coarsely chopped red
   pepper
½ cup water
½ cup olive oil

¼ cup white wine vinegar
2 tablespoons fresh lemon
   juice
1 tablespoon snipped fresh
   parsley
1 clove garlic, minced
1 teaspoon sugar
¼ teaspoon celery seed
¼ teaspoon salt

6 servings

In 2-quart casserole, combine Brussels sprouts, carrots, onion, pepper and water. Cover. Microwave at High for 8 to 12 minutes, or until vegetables are tender-crisp, stirring once or twice. Let stand, covered, for 2 to 3 minutes. Drain. Set aside.

In 2-cup measure, combine remaining ingredients. Pour over vegetable mixture. Toss to coat. Cover. Chill at least 4 hours, or until vegetables are cold and flavors are blended.

Per Serving:			
Calories:	214	Cholesterol:	—
Protein:	3 g.	Sodium:	111 mg.
Carbohydrate:	12 g.	Exchanges:	2½ vegetable, 3½ fat
Fat:	18 g.		

Warm Tomato Platter ▶

2 large tomatoes, cut into
   ¼-inch slices
2 Roma tomatoes, each cut
   into 8 wedges
1 cup yellow or red cherry
   tomatoes, cut in half
2 tablespoons sliced green
   onion
2 tablespoons margarine or
   butter
1 tablespoon snipped fresh
   basil leaves
1 teaspoon packed brown
   sugar
¼ teaspoon salt

4 servings

Arrange tomatoes on 10-inch plate. Sprinkle with onion. Cover with plastic wrap. Microwave at High for 2 to 4 minutes, or until tomatoes are warm to the touch, rotating plate once. Set aside.

In 1-cup measure, microwave margarine at High for 45 seconds to 1 minute, or until melted. Add basil, sugar and salt. Mix well. Drizzle over warm tomatoes. Serve immediately.

Per Serving:	
Calories:	80
Protein:	1 g.
Carbohydrate:	7 g.
Fat:	6 g.
Cholesterol:	—
Sodium:	203 mg.
Exchanges:	1 vegetable, 1 fat

Rosemary Summer Squash Trio

2 cups sliced patty pan squash
1 medium yellow summer squash, cut into 2 × ½-inch spears (about 1 cup)
1 medium zucchini, cut into 2 × ½-inch spears (about 1 cup)
3 tablespoons margarine or butter
1 tablespoon snipped fresh rosemary leaves or 1 teaspoon dried rosemary leaves, crushed
2 teaspoons fresh lemon juice
¼ teaspoon salt

4 to 6 servings

In 2-quart casserole, combine all ingredients. Mix well. Cover. Microwave at High for 6 to 10 minutes, or until vegetables are tender-crisp, stirring twice. Let stand, covered, for 3 minutes. Serve with slotted spoon.

Per Serving:	
Calories:	67
Protein:	1 g.
Carbohydrate:	4 g.
Fat:	6 g.
Cholesterol:	—
Sodium:	153 mg.
Exchanges:	1 vegetable, 1 fat

Summer Squash Scramble

1 cup coarsely chopped onion
2 tablespoons margarine or
  butter
1 clove garlic, minced
½ teaspoon dried basil leaves
¼ teaspoon salt
2 cups sliced zucchini (¼-inch
  slices)
1 cup sliced yellow summer
  squash (¼-inch slices)
2 cups seeded chopped
  tomatoes
1 to 2 tablespoons grated
  Parmesan cheese

4 servings

In 2-quart casserole, combine onion, margarine, garlic, basil and salt. Mix well. Cover. Microwave at High for 3 to 5 minutes, or until onion is tender, stirring once.

Add squash. Toss gently to combine. Re-cover. Microwave at High for 7 to 9 minutes, or until tender-crisp, stirring twice.

Add tomatoes. Toss gently to combine. Re-cover. Microwave at High for 1 to 2 minutes, or until hot. Serve with slotted spoon. Sprinkle each serving with Parmesan cheese.

Per Serving:			
Calories:	107	Cholesterol:	1 mg.
Protein:	3 g.	Sodium:	233 mg.
Carbohydrate:	11 g.	Exchanges:	2 vegetable, 1½ fat
Fat:	7 g.		

Summer
Sweets

Watermelon Glacier Pops
Raspberry Freezer Pops

Quick Pick-Me-Ups

Fruit-filled Freezer Cookies ▶

¼ lb. white or chocolate-
    flavored candy coating
24 assorted cookies (1½ to
    2-inch)

Fresh strawberry slices
Fresh raspberries
Mandarin orange segments

6 servings

Line large baking sheet with wax paper. Set aside. In small mixing
bowl, microwave candy coating at 50% (Medium) for 2 to 4 minutes,
or until coating can be stirred smooth, stirring once. Spoon small amount
of coating onto back of each of 12 cookies.

Place cookies coated-side-up on prepared baking sheet. Arrange 2
or 3 strawberry slices, 4 raspberries or 2 orange segments in coating
on cookie. Spoon small amount of coating over fruit.

Top each cookie with another cookie, pressing lightly to sandwich.
Drizzle remaining coating over cookies. Freeze until set. Place frozen
cookies in large plastic food-storage bag and store in freezer.

Per Serving:			
Calories:	182	Cholesterol:	10 mg.
Protein:	2 g.	Sodium:	57 mg.
Carbohydrate:	25 g.	Exchanges:	1 starch, ½ fruit, 1½ fat
Fat:	8 g.		

Freezer S'more Sandwiches

1 cup hot fudge topping
24 whole graham crackers

1 quart vanilla ice cream

24 ice cream sandwiches

Spread 1 heaping tablespoon topping on bottom side of each of 12
crackers. Arrange crackers fudge-side-up on 15½ × 10½-inch baking
sheet, lining bottom of sheet with crackers. Freeze 15 minutes.

Remove cover from ice cream. Microwave at 50% (Medium) for 45
seconds to 1 minute, or until softened. Spread evenly over topping.
Top with remaining crackers to make sandwiches. Cover with foil.

Freeze until firm, about 8 hours or overnight. Cut along perforations
with sharp knife to yield 24 sandwiches. Wrap each sandwich in foil,
if desired, and freeze.

Per Serving:			
Calories:	141	Cholesterol:	10 mg.
Protein:	3 g.	Sodium:	126 mg.
Carbohydrate:	22 g.	Exchanges:	1½ starch, 1 fat
Fat:	5 g.		

Frozen Fruit Treats

2 lbs. assorted fruits (fresh
strawberries, red or green
grape clusters, canned
drained mandarin orange
segments, fresh grapefruit
or orange segments, fresh
cantaloupe or pineapple
chunks)
¾ lb. white or chocolate-
flavored candy coating
3 teaspoons shortening

8 to 10 servings

Line large baking sheet with wax paper. Arrange fruits in single layer on prepared baking sheet. Freeze fruit at least 3 hours, or until firm.

In medium mixing bowl, combine candy coating and shortening. Microwave at 50% (Medium) for 2½ to 5½ minutes, or until melted, stirring once.

Dip half of each fruit piece in coating. Return coated pieces to baking sheet. Freeze until set. Serve immediately or place dipped fruit pieces in large plastic food-storage bag and store in freezer.

Per Serving:			
Calories:	237	Cholesterol:	6 mg.
Protein:	3 g.	Sodium:	31 mg.
Carbohydrate:	31 g.	Exchanges:	2 fruit, 2½ fat
Fat:	12 g.		

Raspberry Freezer Pops

1 pint vanilla ice cream
1 cup fresh raspberries, divided
6 wax-coated paper drink cups
    (7 oz. each)
1 pint raspberry sherbet
6 flat wooden Popsicle sticks

6 pops

Place ice cream in medium mixing bowl. Cut into quarters. Microwave at 50% (Medium) for 30 seconds to 1 minute, or until softened. Add ½ cup raspberries. Mix gently to combine. Divide half of ice cream mixture evenly among cups. Place remaining mixture in freezer.

Place raspberry sherbet in 2-quart casserole. Cut into quarters. Microwave at 50% (Medium) for 30 seconds to 1 minute, or until softened. Add remaining ½ cup raspberries to sherbet. Mix gently to combine. Spoon half of sherbet mixture evenly over ice cream mixture in cups. Spoon remaining ice cream and sherbet mixtures into cups. Insert stick in center of each cup. Freeze about 4 hours, or until firm. To serve, peel cups from pops.

Gumdrop Pops: Follow recipe above, except substitute ¾ cup gumdrops cut into small pieces for raspberries, and pineapple sherbet for raspberry sherbet.

Per Serving:	
Calories:	190
Protein:	3 g.
Carbohydrate:	33 g.
Fat:	6 g.
Cholesterol:	25 mg.
Sodium:	68 mg.
Exchanges:	1 starch, 1 fruit, 1 fat

Watermelon Glacier Pops ▲

2 slices watermelon
    (1 inch thick)

6 flat wooden Popsicle sticks
¼ to ½ lb. white candy coating

4 to 6 pops

Line baking sheet with wax paper. Set aside. Cut each watermelon slice into 2 or 3 wedges. Using sharp knife, cut slit in center of rind on each wedge. Insert stick. Place on prepared baking sheet. Freeze 3 hours or overnight.

In small mixing bowl, microwave candy coating at 50% (Medium) for 2 to 5 minutes, or until coating can be stirred smooth, stirring once. Hold each pop upright and spoon coating over tips of watermelon wedges. Return to baking sheet. Freeze until firm. Wrap each watermelon pop in foil and freeze.

Per Serving:			
Calories:	154	Cholesterol:	20 mg.
Protein:	2 g.	Sodium:	4 mg.
Carbohydrate:	23 g.	Exchanges:	1½ fruit, 1 fat
Fat:	6 g.		

Spoonable
Soda & Fruit Gel

3½ cups ginger ale, orange,
      lemon-lime or strawberry
      soda
 ¼ cup sugar (optional)
 ½ cup cold water
  2 envelopes (0.25 oz. each)
      unflavored gelatin
  8 clear plastic drink cups
      (10 oz. each)
  8 cups mixed fresh fruits*
      (strawberries, grapes,
      melon balls, blueberries,
      raspberries, peach slices)
  8 plastic spoons

                        8 servings

Measure soda into 8-cup measure. Add sugar. Set aside.

Place water in 2-cup measure.
Sprinkle gelatin over water. Let
stand for 5 minutes. Microwave
at High for 30 seconds to 1¼ minutes, or until gelatin is dissolved,
stirring once. Add to soda mixture. Mix well.

Fill cups to within ½ inch of rim
with fruit. Insert spoons. Add ½
cup gelatin mixture to each cup.
Chill 4 hours, or until set.

*Do not use fresh pineapple or
kiwifruit in gelatin mixture. They
contain enzymes that interfere
with the gelling process.

Per Serving:	
Calories:	107
Protein:	3 g.
Carbohydrate:	25 g.
Fat:	—
Cholesterol:	—
Sodium:	9 mg.
Exchanges:	1½ fruit

Bite-size Freezer Mocha Cups

12 foil midget bake cups (2-inch diameter)
1 container (8 oz.) coffee-flavored low-fat yogurt
⅓ cup miniature semisweet chocolate chips
1 cup prepared whipped topping

12 servings

Place foil cups on baking sheet. Set aside. In medium mixing bowl, combine yogurt and chocolate chips. Fold in whipped topping. Spoon about 2 tablespoons mixture into each baking cup. Freeze about 2 hours, or until firm. Place frozen mocha cups in large plastic food-storage bag and store in freezer.

Per Serving:
Calories: 53
Protein: 1 g.
Carbohydrate: 6 g.
Fat: 3 g.
Cholesterol: 2 mg.
Sodium: 17 mg.
Exchanges: ½ low-fat milk

Cool Dippers

Crushed ice
Salt
3 pints premium ice cream
  (assorted flavors)
36 butter or sugar cookies
3 lbs. assorted fresh fruits
  (strawberries, pineapple
  wedges, melon wedges,
  cherries, red or green
  grape clusters)

12 servings

Per Serving:	
Calories:	287
Protein:	4 g.
Carbohydrate:	40 g.
Fat:	14 g.
Cholesterol:	51 mg.
Sodium:	115 mg.
Exchanges:	1 starch, 1½ fruit, 2½ fat

How to Microwave Cool Dippers

Layer crushed ice and salt, 4 parts ice to 1 part salt, in 13 × 9-inch baking dish.

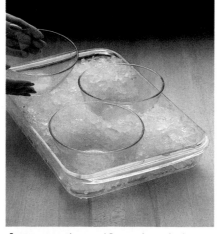

Arrange three 16-oz. bowls in crushed ice. Place in freezer.

Remove lid from 1 pint ice cream. Using scissors, cut down sides of carton; remove ice cream.

Place ice cream in small mixing bowl. Microwave at 30% (Medium Low) for 45 seconds to 1½ minutes, or until ice cream can be stirred smooth, stirring twice.

Spoon softened ice cream into one of the prepared bowls. Repeat with remaining 2 pints of ice cream. Serve with cookies and fresh fruit as dippers.

Cool Desserts

Chocolate-drizzled Dessert Kabobs

4   slices pound cake
        (4 × 2 × ½-inch)
        Raspberry jam or preserves
4   wooden skewers, 8-inch
4   cantaloupe melon balls or
        banana chunks
4   whole fresh strawberries
4   chunks peeled kiwifruit
        (1-inch chunks)
1   square (2 oz.) chocolate-
        flavored candy coating
1   teaspoon shortening

4 servings

Spread 1 side of each slice of
pound cake with jam. Place 2
slices jam-sides-together. Repeat with remaining slices. Cut
each sandwich into quarters to
yield 8 chunks.

On each skewer, thread 1 melon
ball, 1 cake chunk, 1 strawberry,
1 cake chunk and 1 kiwifruit chunk.
Arrange kabobs on wax-paper-
lined baking sheet. Set aside.

In small bowl, place candy coating and shortening. Microwave
at 50% (Medium) for 2 to 3 minutes, or until melted, stirring once.
Drizzle melted candy coating over
kabobs. Chill about 5 to 10 minutes, or until set. Serve immediately, or cover with plastic wrap
and chill up to 2 hours.

Per Serving:	
Calories:	224
Protein:	3 g.
Carbohydrate:	29 g.
Fat:	11 g.
Cholesterol:	57 mg.
Sodium:	102 mg.
Exchanges:	1 starch, 1 fruit, 2 fat

Chocolate Cookies & Cream Squares

24 marshmallow puff cookies
1 quart chocolate ice cream
1 cup coarsely chopped
   walnut halves
1 cup caramel sauce

1 carton (8 oz.) prepared
   whipped topping
12 maraschino cherries with
   stems

12 servings

Arrange cookies in single layer in bottom of 12 × 8-inch baking pan. Set aside.

Place ice cream in medium mixing bowl. Cut into quarters. Microwave at 50% (Medium) for 45 seconds to 1 minute, or until softened. Beat at medium speed of electric mixer until smooth. Spread ice cream evenly over cookies. Sprinkle with nuts.

Freeze about 2 hours, or until firm. Drizzle caramel sauce over ice cream layer. Top with whipped topping. Spread evenly. Garnish with cherries. Freeze about 2 hours, or until firm. Serve in squares.

Per Serving:
Calories:	446	Cholesterol:	47 mg.
Protein:	6 g.	Sodium:	178 mg.
Carbohydrate:	63 g.	Exchanges:	2 starch, 2 fruit, 4 fat
Fat:	21 g.		

Crispy Ice Cream

½ cup flaked coconut
1 cup granola cereal
½ cup miniature semisweet
   chocolate chips
6 scoops ice cream, any flavor
   (3-oz. scoops)

1 cup plus 2 tablespoons
   chocolate-flavored syrup or
   Jamocha Fudge Sauce
   (page 141)

6 servings

Line large baking sheet with wax paper. Set aside. In 8-inch square baking dish, sprinkle coconut in even layer. Microwave at 70% (Medium High) for 3 to 4 minutes, or until lightly browned, tossing with fork after first minute and then every 30 seconds.

Add granola cereal and chocolate chips to coconut. Mix well. Roll each scoop of ice cream in granola mixture. Place on prepared baking sheet. Freeze about ½ hour, or until firm. Spoon 3 tablespoons syrup on individual dessert plates. Place ice cream balls in sauce. Serve immediately.

Per Serving:
Calories:	473	Cholesterol:	30 mg.
Protein:	7 g.	Sodium:	91 mg.
Carbohydrate:	73 g.	Exchanges:	2 starch, 3 fruit, 3 fat
Fat:	21 g.		

Peach Melba Shortcake ▶

1 pkg. (16 oz.) frozen
   unsweetened raspberries
2 teaspoons cornstarch
1 cup whipping cream
1 teaspoon vanilla
2 tablespoons powdered sugar
6 baked buttermilk biscuits (2½
   to 3-inch diameter)
2 to 3 cups sliced fresh peaches
   (two or three 8-oz. peaches)
   Powdered sugar

6 servings

Place raspberries in 2-quart casserole. Cover. Microwave at High for 3 to 5 minutes, or until defrosted. Strain into 4-cup measure. Discard seeds.

Add cornstarch. Blend well with whisk. Microwave at High for 3 to 5 minutes, or until sauce is thickened and translucent, stirring twice. Cover with plastic wrap. Chill about 2 hours, or until cold.

In medium mixing bowl, beat whipping cream and vanilla at high speed of electric mixer until slightly thickened. Continue to beat, gradually adding 2 tablespoons sugar, until soft peaks form. Set aside.

Split biscuits in half horizontally. Spoon about 3 tablespoons sauce on each of 6 individual dessert plates. Place 1 biscuit bottom on each plate.

Spoon 2 tablespoons whipped cream onto each biscuit. Top each evenly with peach slices and 2 tablespoons whipped cream. Replace biscuit tops. Dust tops of biscuits with sugar.

Per Serving:
Calories:	277
Protein:	3 g.
Carbohydrate:	29 g.
Fat:	18 g.
Cholesterol:	54 mg.
Sodium:	235 mg.
Exchanges:	1 starch, 1 fruit, 3½ fat

◄ Brownie Sherbet Pie

1 pkg. (12.9 to 15 oz.) chewy fudge brownie mix
1 pint lemon sherbet
1 pint orange sherbet
1 pint lime sherbet
1 pint raspberry sherbet
⅛ lb. white or chocolate-flavored candy coating

10 servings

Prepare brownie mix as directed on package for traditional brownies. Spread batter evenly in 10-inch deep-dish pie plate. Place in microwave on saucer. Microwave at 50% (Medium) for 6 minutes, rotating once.

Microwave at High for 2½ to 4½ minutes longer, or until wooden pick inserted in center comes out clean and no uncooked batter remains on bottom center, rotating once. (Top surface may appear moist in several areas, but will dry during standing.) Let brownies stand directly on the countertop until completely cool.

Remove cover from lemon sherbet. Microwave at 50% (Medium) for 30 seconds to soften. Spread evenly over brownies. Top with scoops of orange, lime and raspberry sherbet.

In small mixing bowl, microwave candy coating at 50% (Medium) for 2 to 3 minutes, or until coating can be stirred smooth, stirring once. Drizzle over top of pie. Freeze 30 minutes, or until sherbet is firm, but brownie is still soft. Serve in wedges.

Per Serving:	
Calories:	478
Protein:	4 g.
Carbohydrate:	85 g.
Fat:	15 g.
Cholesterol:	40 mg.
Sodium:	238 mg.
Exchanges:	4 starch, 1½ fruit, 2 fat

Melon Sorbet & Cream Pie ▼

⅓ cup margarine or butter
1⅓ cups graham cracker crumbs
2 tablespoons sugar
1 quart vanilla ice cream
2 cups puréed cantaloupe
½ teaspoon grated lime peel
1 tablespoon lime juice
2 drops yellow food coloring
1 drop red food coloring
Whipped cream (optional)
Lime slices (optional)

8 servings

In 9-inch pie plate, microwave margarine at High for 1½ to 1¾ minutes, or until melted. Stir in crumbs and sugar until moistened. Press crumbs firmly and evenly against bottom and sides of pie plate. Microwave at High for 1½ to 2½ minutes, or until crust sets, rotating dish once or twice. Cool completely.

Remove ice cream from carton. Place in medium mixing bowl. Cut into quarters. Microwave at 50% (Medium) for 45 seconds to 1 minute, or until softened.

Add cantaloupe, peel, juice and food colorings. Beat at medium speed of electric mixer until mixture is smooth. Place in freezer. Freeze until mixture is very thick, about 1½ to 1¾ hours, stirring 2 or 3 times.

Mound into prepared crust. Freeze about 4 hours, or until firm. Decorate edges with whipped cream. Garnish with lime slices.

Per Serving:			
Calories:	291	Cholesterol:	30 mg.
Protein:	4 g.	Sodium:	248 mg.
Carbohydrate:	35 g.	Exchanges:	1 starch, 1 fruit, ½ whole milk, 2 fat
Fat:	16 g.		

Checkerboard Truffle

Raspberry Orange Sundae
Sauce (page 141)

Chocolate Layer:
- 1 pkg. (8 oz.) semisweet chocolate baking bars
- ½ cup whipping cream
- ¼ cup butter

White Layer:
- 8 oz. white baking bar
- 1 cup marshmallow cream
- 2 tablespoons whipping cream

16 servings

Per Serving:	
Calories:	284
Protein:	2 g.
Carbohydrate:	37 g.
Fat:	16 g.
Cholesterol:	23 mg.
Sodium:	59 mg.
Exchanges:	2½ fruit, 3 fat

How to Microwave Checkerboard Truffle

Prepare raspberry sauce as directed, except omit gumdrop candies. Cover with plastic wrap and chill until serving time. Line two 8 × 4-inch loaf dishes with plastic wrap. Set aside.

Combine chocolate layer ingredients in medium mixing bowl. Microwave at 50% (Medium) for 4 to 5½ minutes, or until chocolate is melted and mixture can be stirred smooth, stirring twice. Pour evenly into 1 prepared dish. Chill about 4 hours, or until firm.

Combine white layer ingredients in medium mixing bowl. Microwave at 50% (Medium) for 3 to 5½ minutes, or until mixture is melted and can be stirred smooth, stirring after 2 minutes and then every minute. Pour evenly into remaining dish. Chill about 4 hours, or until firm.

Tangerine Soufflé

¼ cup cold water
1 envelope (0.25 oz.)
    unflavored gelatin
4 egg yolks
1 cup sugar
⅔ cup tangerine juice
    concentrate, defrosted
6 drops yellow food coloring
3 drops red food coloring
1½ cups whipping cream
4 egg whites
1 can (15 oz.) mandarin
    orange segments, drained

10 servings

Per Serving:	
Calories:	275
Protein:	4 g.
Carbohydrate:	31 g.
Fat:	16 g.
Cholesterol:	158 mg.
Sodium:	39 mg.
Exchanges:	1½ fruit,
	½ whole milk, 1 fat

Wrap 3-inch strip of aluminum foil around top edge of 1-quart soufflé dish to form collar. Secure with tape. Set aside.

Place water in 1-cup measure. Sprinkle gelatin over water. Let stand for 5 minutes. Microwave at High for 30 seconds to 1¼ minutes, or until gelatin dissolves, stirring once. Set aside.

In medium mixing bowl, combine yolks, sugar and concentrate. Mix well. Microwave at 50% (Medium) for 8 to 10 minutes, or until sugar dissolves and mixture thickens slightly, stirring with whisk 2 or 3 times. Add softened gelatin and the food colorings to yolk mixture. Mix well.

Place bowl of hot mixture in larger bowl containing 1 to 2 inches ice water. Let stand for 15 minutes, or until mixture is slightly thickened, stirring frequently.

Beat whipping cream at high speed of electric mixer until soft peaks form. Gently fold whipping cream into gelatin mixture. Using clean beaters, beat egg whites at high speed of electric mixer until soft peaks form. Gently fold egg whites and orange segments into gelatin mixture. Spoon mixture into prepared soufflé dish. Chill about 4 hours, or until set.

Remove layers from dishes. Cut each in half crosswise. Cut each half lengthwise into 4 strips. Alternate 2 white and 2 dark strips side by side on sheet of plastic wrap. Top first layer with 2 white and 2 dark strips, reversing colors.

Continue layering until complete. Wrap in plastic wrap. Using hands, press loaf gently into a square. Chill until serving time.

Spray knife blade with vegetable cooking spray before slicing. Spoon 2 tablespoons sauce on individual dessert plates. Place slices of truffle in sauce.

◄ Mixed Fresh Fruit Sauce

- 1 tablespoon cornstarch
- 1 cup apricot nectar
- 1 tablespoon lemon juice
- ¼ teaspoon vanilla
- 1 medium fresh peach, cut into chunks (½-inch chunks)
- 1 cup sliced fresh strawberries
- 1 banana, sliced
- 1 kiwifruit, peeled, cut in half lengthwise and sliced

6 servings

Place cornstarch in 1-quart casserole. Blend in apricot nectar, lemon juice and vanilla with whisk until mixture is smooth.

Microwave at High for 3 to 6 minutes, or until sauce is thickened and translucent, stirring once or twice. Cool slightly. Add fruit. Stir gently to combine.

Cover with plastic wrap. Chill about 4 hours, or until cold. Serve sauce over frozen yogurt, ice cream, pound cake or angel food cake.

Per Serving:
Calories:	70
Protein:	1 g.
Carbohydrate:	18 g.
Fat:	—
Cholesterol:	—
Sodium:	2 mg.
Exchanges:	1 fruit

Fresh Mint Sauce ▲

- 1 cup sugar
- 1 cup hot water
- ½ cup fresh mint leaves (½ oz.)
- ¼ cup light corn syrup
- 4 drops green food coloring

16 servings

In 8-cup measure, combine sugar and water. Mix well. Add mint leaves. Microwave at High for 5 to 6 minutes, or until mixture comes to rolling boil, stirring once. Boil for 1 minute.

Strain mixture into 4-cup measure. Discard mint leaves. Add corn syrup and food coloring. Mix well. Cover with plastic wrap. Chill at least 4 hours, or until cold. Serve sauce over ice cream, or as dressing for fruit salads.

Per Serving:
Calories:	63
Protein:	—
Carbohydrate:	16 g.
Fat:	—
Cholesterol:	—
Sodium:	4 mg.
Exchanges:	1 fruit

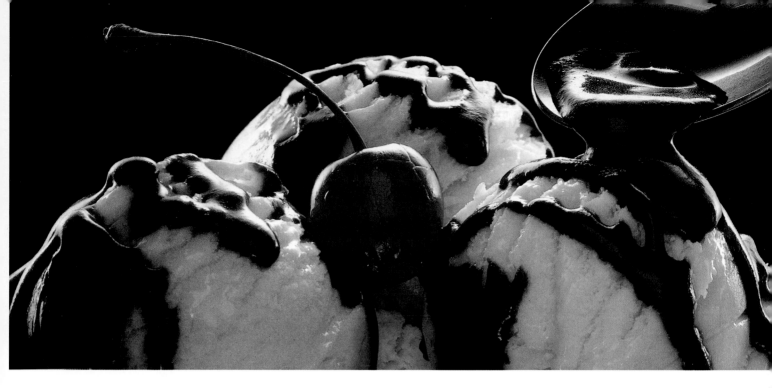

Jamocha Fudge Sauce ▲

3 squares (1 oz. each)
  unsweetened baking
  chocolate
¾ cup packed brown sugar
2 teaspoons instant coffee
  crystals
1 can (12 oz.) evaporated milk
½ teaspoon vanilla
  Slivered almonds

16 servings

In 2-quart casserole, microwave chocolate squares at 50% (Medium) for 4 to 5 minutes, or until melted, stirring twice. Add sugar gradually, stirring with whisk after each addition. Add coffee crystals. Add evaporated milk gradually, stirring with whisk after each addition, until mixture is blended.

Microwave at High for 5 to 10 minutes, or until mixture is thickened and begins to boil, stirring with whisk every 2 minutes. Add vanilla.

Place sheet of plastic wrap directly on surface of sauce. Chill about 2 hours, or until cold. Store in covered container in refrigerator. Serve over ice cream. Sprinkle each serving with almonds.

Per Serving:			
Calories:	94	Cholesterol:	6 mg.
Protein:	2 g.	Sodium:	26 mg.
Carbohydrate:	14 g.	Exchanges:	½ fruit, ½ whole milk
Fat:	4 g.		

Raspberry Orange Sundae Sauce

1 pkg. (16 oz.) frozen
  unsweetened raspberries
1 tablespoon cornstarch
½ teaspoon ground cinnamon
⅔ cup light corn syrup
½ cup orange slice gumdrop
  candies, halved

16 servings

In 2-quart casserole, combine raspberries, cornstarch and cinnamon. Toss to coat. Add corn syrup. Mix well. Microwave at High for 8 to 11 minutes, or until mixture is thickened and translucent, stirring 2 or 3 times. Strain into medium mixing bowl. Discard seeds.

Add gumdrops to strained mixture. Mix well. Chill. Serve sauce over frozen yogurt, ice cream, pound cake or angel food cake.

Per Serving:			
Calories:	75	Cholesterol:	—
Protein:	—	Sodium:	11 mg.
Carbohydrate:	19 g.	Exchanges:	1 fruit
Fat:	—		

MENUS

Summer Fiesta

A fiesta feeling comes naturally with tastes as lively as a jalapeño chili pepper and dishes as colorful as a Guadalajara market.

Summer Entertaining

This menu emphasizes fuss-free entertaining. For the most part, food preparation is completed before guests arrive, leaving everyone free to enjoy the evening to the fullest.

Midsummer Night

A delightfully different entrée, made more elegant with asparagus. This easy summertime meal is completed by adding a refreshing minted salad, a cool glass of Lime Mineral Water and wonderful Crispy Ice Cream.

Summer Luncheon

The unique presentation of this chicken salad makes it a perfect choice for a cool summer luncheon. Add a refreshing glass of Minted Ice Tea, a frosty bowl of soup, croissants and delightful Fruit-filled Freezer Cookies.

By the Beach

Whether your summers are short or long, there is never enough time to savor sunny skies and warm breezes. This menu is ideal for entertaining away from home, giving you time to enjoy summer pleasures.

Backyard Bash

The atmosphere is casual and comfortable, and the gang's all here. So bring on those hearty appetites and dish up a Backyard Bash to remember.

Oriental Porch Party

Enhance the flavor and aroma of charcoal-cooked food by giving it an Oriental flair! With this menu, you can prepare your entrée as well as your dessert on the grill.

Early Spring Supper

Bright and colorful, this main dish is prepared quickly and easily, complemented with fresh fruit and dinner rolls and followed by the grand finale which is grand indeed — super-rich chocolate Checkerboard Truffle.

Summer in the Park

Outdoor barbecuing is definitely a part of summer fun in America. Short preparation time and minimal cleanup are most appealing, so for casual, uncomplicated entertaining, this collection of recipes is perfect.

Garden Splendor

You may call this a "vegetarian delight," but do call it a fresh idea for casual entertaining. "Fresh" it is, featuring garden goodies such as tomatoes, onions, yellow squash and zucchini. Add French bread, Wilted Spinach & Fruit Salad and tasty Fruit Cake Kabobs for a true summer meal.

Patio Party

Without question, summer days are salad days. This salad combines some of summer's best harvest in a colorful happening. Complemented by assorted breads, chilled soup and a cool and refreshingly light dessert.

Summer Fiesta

Iced Tomato Dill Bisque *page 30*

Chicken Fajitas *page 84*   Confetti Corn *page 115*

Ice Cream with Fresh Mint Sauce *page 140*

The day before, or early in the day: Prepare bisque and mint sauce. ***About 3 hours before serving:*** Prepare and marinate chicken. Microwave corn while chicken is grilling. Assemble fajitas. Reheat corn, if necessary.

Backyard Bash

Beer-basted Brats *page 87* Turkey Burgers *page 85* Buns & Condiments
Farmers' Market Potato Salad *page 38* Old-fashioned Lemonade *page 22*
Warm Tomato Platter *page 118* Watermelon Glacier Pops *page 127*

The day before: Prepare and freeze watermelon pops. Prepare and refrigerate potato salad. **Early in the day:** Shape and refrigerate turkey burgers. Prepare and refrigerate lemonade and the tomato platter. **About ½ hour before serving:** Prepare grill. Microwave brats and turkey burgers.

Summer Entertaining

Carrot Vichyssoise *page 30*   Assorted Lettuce Salad
Orange Roughy with Berry-Nut Salsa *page 101*
Rice   Bread Sticks   Sherbet

The day before: Prepare and refrigerate vichyssoise. ***Early in the day:*** Wash and chill salad greens. ***45 minutes before serving:*** Prepare salsa. Cook rice conventionally while fish microwaves.

Oriental Porch Party

Sesame Noodle Salad page 37
Teriyaki Pork Kabobs page 86   *Orange-glazed Pineapple* page 89
Almond & Fortune Cookies

The night before: Prepare and marinate pork. Prepare and refrigerate salad. ***Early in the day:*** Cut and chill vegetables for kabobs and prepare pineapple slices. ***About 1½ hours before serving:*** Prepare glaze for pineapple slices. Microwave vegetables for kabobs. Assemble kabobs. Grill kabobs. During last 7 minutes of grilling time, add pineapple slices.

Midsummer Night

Cold Tuna-stuffed Manicotti *page 103*
Minted Melon & Pineapple Salad *page 55*   Lime-flavored Mineral Water
Crispy Ice Cream *page 134*

The day before: Prepare ice cream balls and fudge sauce. ***Early in the day:*** Prepare stuffed manicotti and the fruit salad.

Early Spring Supper

Dilled Salmon with Tricolored Peppers page 100
Fresh Fruit   *Dinner Rolls*
Checkerboard Truffle page 138

The day before, or early in the day: Prepare and assemble truffle. Prepare raspberry sauce and refrigerate. Cut up and refrigerate fruit. ***About 3 hours before serving:*** Microwave and chill salmon. Prepare and chill pepper mixture.

Summer Luncheon

Dilled Chicken Salad Mold *page 49*   Minted Iced Tea *page 20*

Strawberry-Rhubarb Soup *page 26*

Croissants   Fruit-filled Freezer Cookies *page 124*

The day before: Prepare and freeze cookies. Prepare and refrigerate chicken salad mold. *Early in the day:* Prepare tea. Prepare and refrigerate soup mixtures. *30 minutes before serving:* Unmold chicken salad. Prepare individual servings of soup. Fill glasses with ice.

Summer in the Park

Hamburgers & Hot Dogs   Pesto Potato Salad *page 40*
Citrus Cinnamon Tea *page 20*   Buns & Condiments
Watermelon Slices or Brownies

The day before: Prepare and refrigerate potato salad. *Early in the day:* Prepare tea. Shape and refrigerate hamburgers.

By the Beach

South of the Border Muffuletta page 60

Cold Marinated Corn page 115 *Margarita Fruit Salad* page 55

Cookies or Brownies

The day before: Prepare and refrigerate muffuletta. *Early in the day:* Prepare corn and fruit salad.

Garden Splendor

Garden Marinara Sauce *page 102*

Wilted Spinach & Fruit Salad *page 57* French Bread

Chocolate-drizzled Dessert Kabobs *page 132*

Early in the day: Prepare fruit for salad and kabobs. Peel and chop tomatoes for sauce. ***About 2½ hours before serving:*** Assemble and refrigerate kabobs. ***About 45 minutes before serving:*** Prepare and microwave sauce. Cover to keep hot. While pasta boils conventionally, microwave dressing for salad. Toss salad. Reheat sauce, if necessary.

Patio Party

The day before: Prepare and freeze pie. Prepare and refrigerate soup. ***About 3 hours before serving:*** Prepare and chill salad.

Index